The Return of Scarcity

By the same author

Other People's Money
The Fragile Pattern
Kulinma: Listening to Aboriginal Australians
Trial Balance
A Certain Heritage (co-author)

The Return of Scarcity

Strategies for an Economic Future

H.C. COOMBS

Published in association with
Centre for Resource and Environmental Studies
Australian National University

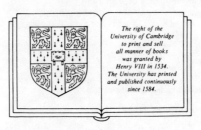

The right of the
University of Cambridge
to print and sell
all manner of books
was granted by
Henry VIII in 1534.
The University has printed
and published continuously
since 1584.

Cambridge University Press

Cambridge
New York   Port Chester   Melbourne   Sydney

Published by the Press Syndicate of the University of Cambridge
The Pitt Building, Trumpington Street, Cambridge CB2 1RP, UK
40 West 20th Street, New York, NY 10011, USA
10 Stamford Road, Oakleigh, Melbourne 3166, Australia

Printed in Australia by Brown Prior Anderson

National Library of Australia cataloguing in publication data:

Coombs, H. C. (Herbert Cole), 1906-   .
  The return of scarcity: strategies for an economic
  future
  Bibliography.
  ISBN 0 521 36373 X.
  ISBN 0 521 36896 0 (pbk.).

  1. Natural resources. 2. Economic development. I. Title.
333.7

British Library cataloguing in publication data:

Coombs, H. C. (Herbert Cole, *1906–*)
  The return of scarcity: strategies for an economic
  future.

  1. Economic policies. Influence of scarcity of
  natural resources

  I. Title

  333.7

  ISBN 0-521-36373-X

Library of Congress cataloguing in publication data:

Coombs, H. C. (Herbert Cole), 1906–
  The return of scarcity.

  Includes bibliographical references.
  1. Economic development—Environmental aspects.
  2. Economic policy. 3. Resource allocation. 4. Natural
  resources—Management. 5. Scarcity. I. Title.
HD75.6.C69   1990   338.9   89–25158
ISBN 0-521-36373-X
ISBN 0-521-36896-0 (pbk.)

We do say that it is the duty and responsibility of the community and particularly those more fortunately placed to see that our less fortunate fellow citizens are protected from those shafts of fate which leave them helpless and without hope; this is the objective for which we are striving. It is, as I have said before, the Beacon: the light on the hill to which our eyes are always turned and to which our efforts are always directed.

Ben Chifley, December 1949

Contents

Introduction

THESE essays have been written for various occasions during the years since my retirement from the Governorship of the Reserve Bank in 1968. Since then my primary concerns have been with policies relating to the arts and the Aboriginal peoples of this continent, and I have refrained from public discussion of issues bearing upon day-to-day economic management. At the same time I have become increasingly conscious of long-term structural changes in our own and the world economy – especially those arising from the interaction of ecological and economic concerns. These essays reflect my anxiety as a private citizen and a member of the academic community about the threat to our society and its future arising from the failure of economic and political analysis to deal effectively with those long-term problems occasioned by that interaction. Collectively the essays attempt to identify the origins and nature of those problems and to explore what simple economic theory can contribute to the design of policies which might mitigate their impact.

Being written about closely related topics but at different times for different audiences and occasions, there is overlap and repetition in the various chapters and some inconsistencies and contradictions and, no doubt, simple errors. No attempt has been made to remove these. There is, I believe, some advantage in presenting them substantially in their original form as a record of changes in thinking in response to developments in external events and to the influence of contemporary views of others sharing the same concerns.

The essays have been written for general readers. The economics used is of the simplest and requires no familiarity with the sophisticated theorems of contemporary models, and I have tried to keep the language free of jargon. In this I have sought to follow the writings of the 'classical' period: of Adam Smith, Ricardo, Marx, Malthus and J.S. Mill who were intelligent generalists rather than professional economists.

Only the first essay, 'Towards a Sustainable Society', has been written for this publication in an attempt to express the present (1989) state of my views about these problems and the options open to us. Logically this should have been the final chapter but it is believed that at the beginning it helps demonstrate the contemporary urgency of the issues with which the book deals and the relevance of the latter chapters to their understanding.

The only departure from the decision to present the essays in the form in which they were first written is in Chapter 8 which integrates two addresses given in the same year, one in Perth and the other in Brisbane. These dealt with substantially the same topics, and to have presented them separately would have increased the repetition and added little to their impact.

The order of the chapters, except for the first, is roughly chronological, but attempts to group the papers coherently in relation to the major issues. Thus Chapters 2-6 deal with areas of conflict or difficulty in reconciling economic and ecological concerns. Chapter 7 is an attempt to assess how those concerns bear upon the quality of human life. Chapter 8 comments on the performance of our political system in dealing with these issues. Chapter 9 explores possible political and economic strategies directed to the achievement of a sustainable society.

I am grateful to those concerned for permission to publish the essays in this form: to the Centre for Resource and Environmental Studies of the Australian National University for the home and service they have provided for me, to Diane Smith and Ettie Oakman and other colleagues in the Centre for their generous help, and to Cambridge University Press and Cathryn Game for their skill and patience with a difficult text.

1

Towards a Sustainable Society

INTRODUCTION – PURPOSES AND CONSTRAINTS

A long-term economic strategy should take account of:

- the social purposes which the economic system can be expected to achieve or to promote, and
- the major changes in the structure and operation of the system which, at least for the present, must be taken as given: changes which may derive from the internal working of the system itself or from the material and social context, national and international, within which it is operating.

The contemporary economic system is an historical artefact; it has developed over time from earlier simpler organisations. Its development can be traced back to the seasonal activities of the hunter-gatherers moving through their territory, to their division of functions within the family and the clan and to their ceremonial and ritual exchanges of scarce and valued resources and properties across tribal and language frontiers. It has, on the way, passed through the peasant, village economy based on largely self-sufficient domestic agriculture, pasturing on common land and home-based handicrafts and through the various stages of the Industrial Revolution.

1

Despite enormous increases in the range, content and organisational complexity of the system, the basic social purposes of economic activity remain the same. The prime social concern of hunter-gathering, of nomadic pastoralism, of peasant land use and of the contemporary industrial economic system has been and is to provide the members of the relevant social group or groups with access to a livelihood; to the material, social, intellectual and (to a degree) spiritual means to a healthy, secure and stimulating life. In this concern the economic system does not function alone. It is an important part – but a part only – of the arrangements of society for the achievement of its common purposes. Judgement of the effectiveness of our own or any economic system, therefore, must be based on how far it contributes to the achievement of these purposes, or how far its operation prevents or handicaps their achievement. Measurements of quantities – of output, of profits, of accumulated wealth, of resources used – are useful aids to policy and management, but the end products of the system are qualitative – the health, security and the lifestyle of the members of the society.

These will be influenced by factors other than the flow of goods and services through the market-place. They will be influenced by the physical and social environment in which the lifestyle is lived, by the experiences (including the work experience) it offers and, above all, by the quality and richness of the cultural experience and personal relationships it makes possible. The fact that these are not readily measurable does not mean that they can be ignored. It is possible to compare as well as to count; to place complex combinations of factors in an assessed order of preference.

THE CHANGING CONTEXT

Contemporary social institutions, including the economic system, function in a world of change. Today change is more rapid and more all-pervading than in the times when those institutions were developed. From the economic point of view the most important contemporary change is what these essays have called 'the return of scarcity' – the effect of an explosively increasing world population confronting finite,

2

material resources which we had come to believe were, for practical purposes, inexhaustible.

This confrontation has been intensified by changes on the side of demand for resources additional to those arising from the simple increase in numbers of human beings. The first of these additional changes is that human ingenuity backed by science and technology has created a vast repertoire of consumers' equipment used in, and diversifying, almost every aspect of living. The components of this repertoire daily seem to become more complex and resource-intensive and yet more essential or desirable in the eyes of most consumers.

Quantitatively the most influential component of this repertoire is the vast armoury of weapons now regarded by the military establishment as vital to national security. Nations, especially the 'super powers' and those who would emulate them, spend annually more on 'defence' and 'security' than was spent on major wars in the past. This expenditure imposes a demand for resources and for accumulated capital, overwhelming that of more constructive purposes, and diverting into its service a disproportionate part of the creativeness and ingenuity of scientists and technologists.

Science and technology, it is true, serve also to ease some of the problems of scarcity. Their work can extend the range of natural resources by sophisticated methods of search and recovery and economise them by better methods of use and by improved recycling.

Science and technology also have profound effects on the methods used in the production of goods and services – both those essential to human survival and those now conventionally thought necessary. These changes in the modes of production have transformed and continue to transform the work experience of those engaged in it, sometimes with deleterious health, social and psychological effects. They also influence the content of education and the whole process of socialising the young in ways which appear to subordinate the full development of their human potential to their suitability as instruments of contemporary technological production and consumption. Most importantly, technological change reduces the need for active human involvement in many productive processes and, therefore, reduces also the capacity of those dependent on employment in enterprises owned

3

and managed by others to find employment and so to command a share of the yield of those enterprises. In a context in which the majority of the population have little property or access to resources, this can mean that those most dependent can be excluded from the means to a livelihood except from charity or government social security programs. Another aspect of this domination of the modes of production by non-human technologically designed instruments is that it too, like the development of consumers' equipment, greatly increases the demand for materials and for capital.

The fourth major source of change is the progressive integration of smaller economies into those of the major economic powers and the emergence of a world economy which transcends even those powers. This world economy is increasingly dominated by transnational corporations, the largest of which exercise power on a scale which dwarfs that of many 'sovereign' states. This source of change is the culmination of a process which began with the colonisation of the lands of the New World. Those countries of Europe which had led the way in the Industrial Revolution and in the 'discovery' of the new lands had the accumulated capital and the military technology to seize control of the new resources and to incorporate them and their previous owners into the European economies. That leadership, and the distribution of accumulated wealth and of military power between these colonising powers, have changed over the subsequent centuries and especially during recent decades. However, the pattern (sometimes called 'neo-colonialism') is essentially the same, and the subordination of the colonised progressively has become more absolute.

The world is still divided between colonisers and colonised in gradations between super powers at one extreme and 'banana republics' at the other. What is new is the falling number of states which exercise significant independent control of their own economic development and choice of lifestyle, and the degree to which the role of colonisers is now performed by transnational corporations which bridge the boundaries and evade the control of even the largest of the nation states.

Within many individual states the pattern of colonisers and colonised is repeated in the increasing polarisation of wealth and power between personal and corporate owners of capital and resources, and

4

those dependent on their capacity to provide labour and services for enterprises owned by others. Similarly, it recurs between those colonisers and their dependants who have taken up residence and property within the colonised territory and the survivors of the indigenous original inhabitants.

EFFECTS OF CHANGE ON THE ECONOMIC SYSTEM

The rise in populations, the increasing scarcity of basic resources, the growing dominance of complex 'equipment' on the conduct of human life and the importance of science-based technology on the modes of production: all exercise important influence on the operation of the economic system. Firstly, they all tend to increase the importance of accumulated capital in the conduct of production. Secondly, they all enable scarce basic resources, technology and capital to command higher prices (including interest as the price of capital) and these increases are likely to exceed reductions in prices due to improved technology and increased efficiency, so that a trend towards continuously upward general price levels is likely. Thirdly, these changes in relative prices will affect the distribution of income and wealth in favour of owners and away from organisers, providers of services and workers. Fourthly, the integration of smaller economies into those of the larger colonising powers and the world economy itself, the concentration of accumulated wealth by members of those economies, and the redistribution of income following these changes, will combine to intensify the domination of the colonisers and the domestic elites among the colonised who identify with and share their power.

The incidence of these effects within and between individual economies will not only depend strongly on the distribution of ownership of the factors of production, especially capital, but also on the institutional structure of the economy concerned. There have been dramatic changes in that structure and in the distribution of power within it.

Some classical economists lived in times when scarcities were a more immediate threat than they became following the colonisation and exploitation of the New World. They foresaw some of these effects and feared that in due course the capitalist system could be faced with a crisis. These economists' model of the economic system was based on

5

the assumption that production would continue to be organised in a number of relatively small-scale competitive enterprises owned, managed and predominantly financed by individual capitalists. Economists feared that competition between these entrepreneurial capitalists facing the rising costs of increasing scarcity would find their profits so reduced as to destroy the incentive to establish or expand enterprises.

To some degree at least, their fear has been countered by the increasing scale and changing corporate structure of contemporary enterprises, which classical economists did not foresee. Corporations now can concentrate various forms of ownership within their collective control. They provide from current earnings a larger proportion of their own increasing capital needs than a small enterprise can hope to do and they have stronger access to institutional sources. The entrepreneurial functions of assessing and identifying opportunity, and organising the various factors of production and marketing effectively, are now performed by employees whose competitively determined rewards can decline without necessary detriment to those of the proprietor. Similarly, corporations can bring within their own control much of the process of technological innovation, pre-empting its ownership to themselves. Likewise they can, by advertising and frequent minor design changes, to some degree maintain for themselves the monopoly rewards of innovation.

The trend which the classical economists feared appears to be evident within industries like agriculture where individual working proprietors face declining rewards, or are being 'proletarianised' into contract farming or other components of agro-business, whose ownership and/or control is predominantly external to the productive enterprise itself. This separation of ownership and control from the process of production means also a personal divorce of decision-makers from the land itself. Increasingly, this has been reflected in a deterioration of husbandry, a lack of concern for the future of the land and finally its degradation and destruction. Similar trends are evident in forestry and fishing, and indeed all the industries which have grown out of the natural productivity of the earth.

The trend to 'proletarianisation' is also evident in the professions and occupations which previously have been the preserve of the self-employed or members of specialised institutions with long-established traditions of independence. Legal and medical practitioners previously practising as individuals, but with the status and protection provided by membership of traditional professional bodies, are increasingly becoming salaried employees. Universities and other centres of learning and research are no longer seen as communities of independent scholars but as employed or supported agencies of the state or large corporations, for the training of the skilled employees those organisations will need and for the conduct of their research and development functions. The role of these institutions as the source of independent analysis of all aspects of human life and of intellectual and moral innovation is subordinated by government policy to the short-term needs of corporate profit.

Whether, and how soon, these trends will affect even the conglomerate corporations and produce the declining profits and incentives which the classical economists feared is uncertain. However, it seems inevitable that the trends will, in the meantime, add to the dominance of commercial corporations in the conduct of the economic system and to the proletarianisation of occupations previously independent. The corporation's multiple sources of ownership rewards will enable it to maintain its dominant position at least for some time.

The extent of this domination is illustrated by the way in which the banking system facilitates the concentration of ownership by the support it gives to takeover bids based on unrealistic expectations that the extravagant and greedy hopes of stock exchange speculators will be justified. Similarly, the influence of major corporations on governments and their policies is strong and increasing. Some governments even feel themselves justified in using public resources to protect large corporations from failure arising from the effects of unwise borrowing and speculation.

In summary, the changes described above in the relationship of population to finite resources and in the internal and international structure of the economic system will show themselves in:

- rising relative prices for natural resources and other factors of production with a 'monopoly' component, and a persistent trend towards higher prices generally;
- historically high interest rates;
- increasing shares of the rewards from production going to owners of resources, capital and technology;
- decreasing bargaining power and declining shares in rewards of enterprises to suppliers of services and of labour;
- increasing shares of the proceeds of ownership going to corporate and other owners in the 'colonising' powers, and to transnational corporations, with increasing domination by them of the development of other economies; and
- increasing difficulty in satisfying the social expectation of adequate and improving real incomes and quality of life for non-owners within populations generally.

Sometimes the emergence of these effects can be delayed or obscured by short-term factors. Thus a basic shortage of a particular resource can be temporarily countered by new discoveries or technological improvements in use practices. Even more importantly it can be suppressed by the anxiety of governments and resource owners in weaker economies to sell. Such anxiety can reflect a desire to sustain economic activity and corporate income in the face of similar anxieties among competitors, and sometimes the need to service public and corporate debt and to maintain payments to shareholders abroad. Such characteristically 'weak' bargaining is common in economies heavily dependent on resource exports.

Similarly governments in such countries have been and still are so desperate to stimulate development by exploitation of resources that they have disposed of the community's land and access to its resources at prices which bear no relationship to their capital value or their potential to add to the long-term national product. Indeed they go further and offer tax concessions, expert services and infrastructure at the cost of the taxpayer and to the detriment of future generations' rights in the resources themselves.

INFORMATION AND POLICY

The way in which some economic information is presented often disguises the fact and the effects of such short-sightedness. For example, the output of a mining enterprise is recorded as income in the gross domestic product and the exports of the country within which the mine is located. In fact it is possible that most of its proceeds could accrue to citizens of other countries. Labourers can be transported great distances to work in the mines and much of their wages remitted to their homes. Supplies and equipment are often imported, as are technology, specialist accounting, engineering, organisational and other services. Debenture and equity capital is often raised abroad and indeed the ownership of the enterprise itself may be wholly or predominantly external. An analysis of the effects of the enterprises on the government and people of the region or country in which the mine operates would require access to the details of expenditure including payments of taxation, interest and debt service charges, dividends and other shareholders' benefits as well as payments for labour, materials and equipment. Many of these data are rarely available. But enough is known to indicate that it is naive to assume that economic development in a particular region or country will be wholly, predominantly or even significantly to the economic benefit of the citizens, other enterprises or government of the region or country.

Similarly, the output of extractive industries (such as mining and forestry) and many other forms of land use are recorded as income for statistics relating to domestic production and/or to international payments. In fact such enterprises often result in the depletion and/or sale of capital assets and so progressively reduce the national wealth and its capacity to sustain the citizens of the future. As Repetto (1985) has pointed out, at present many of our economic statistics are providing our business leaders and our governments with misleading signals. Those statistics should be recast at least to make clear how far the proceeds are in fact used or available to create other capital assets, or how far their distribution represents a net reduction in the nation's capital assets.

INCOME DISTRIBUTION – DOMESTIC AND INTERNATIONAL

The degree to which those proceeds will flow to individuals, corporations and governments of a particular country will depend on:

- the degree to which its members own, finance or help finance the enterprises exploiting its resources;
- the degree to which its members own the rights to technology employed in the economy's enterprises or those of other economies;
- the degree to which its members are able from accumulated wealth or current savings to finance the country's new or expanding enterprises; and
- the degree to which its government is able by taxation, royalty charges and similar means to extract for its purposes, and those of the community, a share of the proceeds of the enterprises concerned.

It is clear that colonising powers whose citizens and corporations have established controlling ownership interests in much of the world's resources, who have built up accumulations of financial assets, who frequently are leaders in technological development and owners of patent and other rights in it, are well placed to maintain or strengthen their claims on the proceeds of economic activity round the world.

Other nations which have sources of scarce resources within their borders and which have been able to retain ownership could similarly benefit. However, even when basic property remains with such nations they frequently find it necessary to share their monopolistic advantage with others. Thus, for instance, the Middle East oil producers appear to have shared the benefits of the 1973 price rise with the international oil corporations, and Australia shares the benefits of its mineral wealth with transnational mining corporations.

In summary, economies are in the best position to benefit from or to avoid disadvantage from increasing scarcities to the degree that:

- their resource industries are owned by their own citizens;
- they are able to finance the development of their own enterprises from their domestic savings;

10

- the technology employed in their enterprises is owned by their own members; and
- they are not 'anxious' sellers on international markets.

At first glance Australia seems to be well placed to benefit from increasing scarcities of basic resources. The land is rich in minerals and in fossil and nuclear fuels. It has extensive lands which produce variable but substantial surpluses of foodstuffs and raw materials available for export. It has had high standards of education and an effective record of scientific and technological innovation.

Unfortunately, judged by the above criteria, Australian citizens, corporations and governments have failed to realise the potential of these advantages. Many major enterprises are subsidiaries of overseas firms or are dominated by their links with such firms. Much of the loan and equity capital employed, particularly in mining and other extractive industries, is raised abroad. Technology and expertise are hired from these sources also. Even where Australian research or innovation has been the source of new technology, it frequently passes into foreign ownership as the price of access to significant external markets.

Not until major enterprises are required to publish the details of their expenditure, classified to make clear the location of the recipients and the productive factors to which it is directed, will it be possible to assess confidently how wisely we are using and protecting the resources the land is blessed with.

Not until our national accounts cease classifying exports of exhaustible resources as income and treat them as the sale of capital assets, reducing our national wealth and impairing our economic future, will our business managers, economists and politicians receive accurate signals about the health of our economy.

AUSTRALIA'S RESPONSE TO ECONOMIC CHANGE

But even with present information it can be said with reasonable confidence that from the point of view of the social purposes for which the economic system exists and its long-term sustainability, the Australian economy is open to the following criticisms:

1. It is running down our national capital in natural resources

11

without the proceeds being used to create, on a comparable scale, other capital assets for sustainable production.

2. The industries concerned are generally highly capital-intensive, draw on expensive foreign-owned technology and expertise and expand our need for capital to levels which can be met only with high interest rates and dependence on external sources. The capital cost per job created in them is often disproportionately high. They are unduly dependent on external sources of capital threatening our capacity to manage our own affairs and even potentially threatening to reduce Australia to the status of a 'banana republic', but it would be ludicrous to apply that judgement to public indebtedness only. The servicing of private corporate external debt and dividend payments must be met from proceeds of domestic production in just the same way as that of external public debt. From the point of view of independence, private corporate debt is probably even more intrusive as the policies of the relevant corporations in Australia become increasingly subordinated to the interests of their external associates.

3. For its levels of gross national production Australian savings are inadequate for the rate of economic growth envisaged and much of them are directed to unproductive consumers' equipment. Tax concessions to upper and corporate incomes are often reflected in conspicuous extravagance or in bidding up the price of existing properties, rather than in higher levels of productive investment.

4. Technological change, concentration of enterprises and the increasing rewards for owners – as compared with providers – of services and labour are making it increasingly difficult to meet the reasonable expectations of wage and salary earners. Despite steady, if unspectacular, increases in aggregate domestic production the real incomes of these people, the unemployed dependent families and the aged have been declining over the last decade or more. This trend seems likely to continue.

5. Gross inequalities in the distribution of income combined with extravagant expenditure (often at the taxpayers' expense) on advertising are contributing to a pattern of consumption much

12

marked by conspicuous waste and extravagance, while lower income earners, the aged and the unemployed in increasing numbers face poverty.

6. The obsession with small government in the interests of big business is making it increasingly difficult for governments to perform essential functions the private sector cannot or is unwilling to perform. Public assets and amenities and environmental quality deteriorate, pollution mounts, the quality and accessibility of education declines. We become increasingly dependent on foreign private industry for scientific and technological progress at mounting cost to our balance of payments.

7. The imposition of commercial values and objectives on the educational system and the attacks on the independence of those institutions to which we must look for intellectual creativity and social and moral regeneration are progressively destroying the sources from which a healthier, more humane society can grow.

To check, let alone to reverse, these tendencies will not be easy. The action required would run counter to the ideologies which dominate our political parties, the media, business leaders and trade unions, and increasingly those who determine the structure and purposes of our education systems and our centres of intellectual and cultural innovation.

It will, it seems to me, be necessary for us

- to abandon the conviction that 'bigger is better' and to qualify seriously the belief that maximum growth is the *sine qua non* of economic wisdom;
- to establish sustainability as the primary objective for enterprises exploiting or using natural resources;
- to aim for a rate of economic development which can be financed from our own domestic savings, and preferably which permits a gradual reduction in foreign ownership and external indebtedness, public and private;
- to devote intelligence and resources to developing our own science and technology and their application – especially to those aspects

13

directed to sustainable sources of energy and to reducing the material and resource content of what we produce and consume;

- to promote attitudes and behaviour which value simplicity and frugality and deprecate ostentation and waste;
- to increase the intellectual, cultural and social components of our desired lifestyle, at the expense of the material possessions; and generally
- to make access to a healthy, stimulating and dignified lifestyle for all citizens the prime objective of economic policy, and to regard the assessment of the numbers of citizens to whom this access is denied or inadequate as the primary indicator of economic success or failure, rather than any aggregate or average of material production or money income.

SOME POSSIBLE CHANGES OF DIRECTION

The actions suggested below would, I believe, contribute to the achievement of a society more consistent with this objective.

Control of Exports of Exhaustible Resources

The export of exhaustible resources, being a reduction in the country's national wealth and domestic employment opportunities and the rights of future generations, should be permitted only where a substantial part of the proceeds is to be employed in the creation of other capital assets of comparable social value. Corporations wishing to export exhaustible resources such as minerals and fuels should obtain an export licence only after a social and economic impact assessment has been conducted in public by a judicial authority. The corporation should be required to submit information including estimates of prospective use of proceeds domestically and internationally to create capital assets for sustainable purposes.

To enforce this requirement a special capital asset replacement royalty or resources tax on the export of exhaustible resources should be imposed, and the proceeds allocated to a special fund for investment in sustainable enterprises. A rebate of this royalty or tax could be granted for payments by the corporation concerned into a trust fund, under its own control, for investment in Australia for sustainable production, or grants to an approved institution for the conduct of scientific and technological research.

Similarly enterprises engaged in agriculture, pastoralism, forestry, fishing, or other resource uses capable of depleting the productivity of the land or seas concerned should be subject to a similar regeneration tax. The tax could be rebated to those which have submitted to an appropriate conservation authority a land use or similar plan which that authority certifies provides adequately for the effective regeneration and/or conservation of the land or waters being used. The certificate of the authority should be subject to renewal periodically after examination of the land concerned.

Savings and Investment

At present governments rely upon tax policies which leave with higher income earners and corporations a substantial margin of untaxed income, in the expectation that a major part of this margin will be saved and used or be available for investment. This rationale, presumably, underlies the generous limits imposed on marginal tax rates and similar concessions to corporations. Superficial observation suggests that these concessions are as likely to lead to extravagant expenditure on consumption and its associated equipment. There is a strong case for a development tax or compulsory savings levy, especially on corporations, with generous rebates for expenditure on increased financial assets. Such a rebatable tax would reward those who actually save, without impairing their freedom to allocate their savings as they wish, while ensuring that corporations and the wealthy in fact perform the social function of capital accumulation.

The demands of large-scale highly capital-intensive enterprises, especially in the field of minerals and fuel, place heavy pressure on domestic savings. This is reflected in higher interest rates, and encourages the sale of exhaustible assets to foreign interests to the detriment of future domestic incomes and economic independence. The social and economic impact assessments proposed above in relation to the export of exhaustible resources would provide the opportunity to

15

examine the impact of the demand for capital from such enterprises on the needs of sustainable industries and of the public generally for costly consumers' capital such as housing and community facilities. There is no doubt that very high interest rates have handicapped the development and sometimes the survival of rural and manufacturing enterprises, to the detriment of the balance of the productive economy and the employment opportunities it offers. There is a strong case for requiring such impact studies in the interests of maintaining appropriate diversity in the structure of the economy, as well as for other economic and social reasons.

These measures may modify – but will not change – the trend of increasing scarcity and its corollary effect of increasing rewards to ownership at the expense of those which flow to the providers of services and labour. These trends derive from the monopoly component that scarcity creates for the bargaining power of ownership and, as J.S. Mill observed, this monopoly power cannot be prevented in a market economy but could, in theory at least, be reserved for the community's benefit. Only if this were done could we counter the long-term decline of the bargaining power of wage earners and others, the increasing industrial and social tension and the personal disillusionment which must result from that decline.

To ensure that the monopoly power of ownership is exercised in trust for the community benefit, action could be taken to:

- reassert, and where necessary re-establish, the public ownership of the natural resources of the continent, its minerals, forests, seas, soils, vegetation and wildlife;
- vest title in these resources in an authority independent of corporate and political control;
- empower that authority to grant licences for the use of these resources only on terms which will ensure their conservation, regeneration and sustainable development, and which will provide a rent determined by tender in a competitive market, so as to return to the authority a major proportion of any monopoly rent the resources extract from the consumer;
- empower the authority to carry out or support research programs

16

designed to develop the potential of these resources on a sustainable basis.

The income from the sale of licences and other sources could be transferred to a separate fund for its social use and distribution. This fund could perhaps be called the Community Estate or the Common Wealth Estate. It could be empowered to use its resources to:

- help finance community-controlled facilities providing services designed to improve and diversify the community's quality of life;
- support research and development designed to conserve and enrich the Estate; or
- distribute a national dividend paid equally to all citizens.

This fund could be supplemented by the proceeds of public enterprises and taxes on capital, especially death and inheritance taxes. The aim of the latter should be to transfer progressively to community ownership (perhaps in the form of non-voting shares) a substantial part of the community's corporate wealth. This could be achieved by inheritance taxes by which, above a substantial maximum, only a life interest in income from capital assets could be transferred to heirs.

Wages, Competitiveness and Standards of Living

The effects of restoring community ownership could ease the problems which face industry and its employees in relation to wages and the need to be competitive. Government and trade union collaboration through the Accord has enabled a reduction in real wages and substantial changes in work practices in the interests of competitiveness, so far without serious industrial and social strife. This is a significant achievement, but the pressure from industry for further reductions has not relaxed, and domestic and international pressure for the removal of constraints on international specialisation and competition suggests that that pressure will be intensified, irrespective of its effects on real income and on poverty. The effects of such specialisation and competition will be to bring greater equality between the rewards in different countries of the various factors of production including labour. Increasing equality in the rewards of labour will be achieved by reduc-

17

tions in those relatively high, rather than by increases in those at the lower end of the scale.

The increasing role of transnational corporations in enterprises of national economies means that these enterprises will be restructured to direct their various phases of production to the cheapest and most acquiescent source of labour. One example is the fact that Australian publishing houses (an industry dominated by foreign corporations) export most of their printing to South-east Asian centres.

One obvious response for wage policy would be to abolish the indefensible pay-roll tax and offset the revenue lost by increasing taxes which fall on profits, or alternatively by imposing a tax on energy use. It is stupid to handicap the use of labour and to increase prices by such a tax when inflation continues and real incomes of wage earners are declining, and when the numbers unemployed and/or outside the workforce are increasing. A tax on non-renewable energy use would encourage economies and innovation in an ecologically important area. It would be simple to administer and its proceeds could be used to support the development of sustainable energy resources and other capital purposes.

To increase the share of the rewards of ownership flowing to those on low incomes through measures like those described above would help protect them from the impact of a continuing decline in their industrial bargaining power. It would also enable the scope of the Accord to be widened to cover all components contributing to the level of real income and quality of life.

Lifestyle, Planning, Advertising Etc.

The problem of poverty is intensified by the unnecessary complexity of lifestyles available. There are communities in the world which offer healthy, stimulating and dignified lives on incomes lower even than those we would regard as 'below the poverty line' (although their number is declining as they are incorporated into the world economy). Many of the 'needs' of Australian citizens reflect accepted standards imposed by law, convention, fashion or advertising rather than the requirements of health, morality or livelihood. The influences which shape those standards are more often the desire to stimulate the scale

18

and profitability of commercial enterprises than to meet those requirements as simply, efficiently and as cheaply as possible.

In this the advertising industry is a major influence. It is concerned to
encourage expenditure and to direct it rather than to provide consumers with information about what is available and to enable
informed use of their resources. Much advertising is purely competitive;
to influence and defend the market share of particular 'brand' products
against others often, for all practical purposes, identical. It serves, therefore, no significant social purpose. It is ridiculous that advertising
expenditure which is in essence a capital expenditure to build or defend
the 'good will' of the enterprise concerned should be chargeable as a
cost in assessing its taxable income. Indeed, to do so is of doubtful
professional propriety if not legality. There is a strong case for setting
percentage maximum limits to the expenditure on advertising eligible
as 'costs' and for excluding all those forms of it which are not directed to
providing consumer information. Expenditure on political propaganda,
or on image building, should not qualify.

The planning of cities, suburbs, towns and neighbourhoods could
contribute much to the real income available to all their residents irrespective of income if they were conceived as locations for living which
enabled human activities to be conducted simply, with minimum
expensive capital equipment, and economically, especially in relation to
energy.

CONCLUSION

There is nothing inherently impracticable in these proposals. They
would preserve an economic system based upon private (largely corporate) ownership of economic enterprises motivated by profit and the
accumulation of personal and corporate wealth. They would be helped
if captains of industry were less attracted to conspicuous and extravagant consumption, and if the community generally saw virtue in simplicity and frugality. But it need not destroy the attractions of wealth
nor require a monastic or Buddhist lifestyle among the community
generally. They could be implemented without expropriation, revolution or even major constitutional reform. On the other hand, they
could check the increasing polarisation of our society and the growing

19

domination of our lives and our institutions by the values of speculators and exploiters.

Their chances of being applied are slender while the domination of those values continues and while its ideologies guide our political and economic action. However, that domination is increasingly being questioned by those who see its destructive impact on the physical and social environment in which the destiny of humankind inevitably must be worked out. These proposals provide a basis for action which could match the economic with the ecological realities of that environment and of our time. They could perhaps provide, for politicians who believe that people matter, new fuel for Ben Chifley's 'light on the hill' which grows pale in the hectic flush of growth at all costs.

2

Scarcity, Wealth and Income

Originally presented as paper when President of the Australian Conservation Foundation, at Hobart, Tasmania, October 1978. Subsequently presented at the Centre for Resource and Environmental Studies, Australian National University, Canberra, ACT, January 1979.

S CARCITY – particularly in relation to the world's non-renewable resources – is becoming an increasingly important factor in the working of the economic system. While a vast flood of economic analysis and speculation has followed the recognition of that scarcity, as reflected in the dramatic increases in 1973 in the world prices of crude oil, little of it has dealt with the effects of that rise on the distribution of the final product of the economic system between the groups of people who compose it. I believe it is the differential effects of such scarcities on the distribution of wealth and incomes between these groups which are already posing and will increasingly pose the most difficult problems and call for the most dramatic revision of human values and expectations.

Classical economists during the nineteenth century devoted a great deal of attention to the way in which the shares of capital, labour and proprietorship of land were determined. In the United Kingdom, where agricultural land tended to be owned by a class of people who did not themselves use it in production but hired it out to farmers, questions about how the rewards of the landowner were determined and whether those rewards were socially justifiable, constituted important elements in economic and political controversies of the time. The similarity

21

between agricultural land and other natural resources was noted but did not receive comparable attention since the limitations of the supply at that time were not so evident. Nevertheless, W.S. Jevons (*The Coal Question*, 1865) recognised that coal, upon which British industry had built its world-wide dominance, was not unlimited and that the same principles would apply to it as to agricultural land as it became more scarce.

In European countries the problem of the reward of proprietors was not so sharply realised since land tended to be owned and productively used by the same persons, so the reward of ownership appeared simply as part of profit. In the event, the colonisation of new lands and consequent exploitation of resources during the eighteenth, nineteenth and early twentieth centuries, together with the internationalisation of the market for resources, pushed the problems of resource scarcity into the background. It has been kept there until recently by continuing discoveries and by the growing conviction that science and technology will always devise adequate and competitive alternatives for any resources whose growing scarcity threatens to become embarrassing.

This conviction is now widely questioned. The joint action of most oil-producing countries in 1973 to increase the price of crude oil, and the inability, at least in the short run, of consuming countries to counter this increase, appeared to lend market authority to the warnings about the increasing pressure on the finite resources of this our 'Spaceship Earth' by rising population and increasing material production. Debate between doomsayers and those who pin their faith on technology and market prices has intensified.

In the light of this more recent experience, it may be appropriate to return to the questions posed by classical economists of how the rewards of ownership of scarce resources are determined; to consider how those rewards will be affected by increasing scarcity; to assess what will follow for the rewards of the other active participants in production and to judge what effects these changes will have on the pattern of our society and its capacity to satisfy our notions of social justice.

The classical doctrine on the rewards of ownership of scarce resources can be summarised in the three following quotations from

22

John Stuart Mill's *Principles of Political Economy* (1848 and 1852):

> The only person, beside the labourer and the capitalist, whose consent is necessary to production and who can claim a share of the produce as a price of that consent, is the person who, by the arrangements of society, possesses exclusive power over some natural agent. The land is the principal natural agent . . . and the consideration paid for its use is called rent.
>
> . . . rent is the effect of a monopoly; though the monopoly is a natural one, which may be regulated, which may even be held as a trust for the community generally but which cannot be prevented from existing.
>
> The rent, therefore, which any land will yield, is the excess of its produce, beyond what would be returned to the same capital if employed on the worst land in cultivation. . . . competition, which equalises the profits of different capitals, will enable the landlord to appropriate it [that is, the excess].

In other words, classical economists envisaged land and other similar natural resources as each being capable – because of their intrinsic qualities: proximity, ease and cheapness of access – of being arranged in order of their usefulness to any particular form of production. The least useful commands a price which just covers the cost of rewarding, at competitive rates, the labour and capital required to make it available. Owners of the more useful will be able, because of the scarcity of the resource, to demand of an organiser of production whatever surplus over the standard reward of capital that he may in fact be able to earn.

Subsequent developments, since the classical economists taught on these lines, have somewhat modified theoretical expositions about the nature and significance of rent. It became clear that there were many components of production other than land to which much the same principles applied, which were variable in their usefulness, could be arranged in order of that usefulness, and the ownership of which conferred a monopoly power on its possessor. This power enabled its owner to extract from the organiser of production a share of the product in recognition of the superiority of the owner's component over the least useful available to that organiser.

23

Thus it became apparent that not only natural resources like land, forests and minerals were scarce enough for some to command a 'rent'. Ownership or control of patents and details of technological processes, of personal knowledge, skills and aptitudes, of political and other power or influence, and of exceptional organisational capacities, could all confer power to demand a share of the final product. As productive processes became more complex opportunities to demand such a share spread more widely and were derived from increasingly varied elements used in production. Indeed it is the element of scarcity, natural or contrived, in these elements which enables rewards to continue above the minimum or standard return to labour and capital rather than being eliminated by competition. It is not too much to say that, in industrialised society, the final income enjoyed by any persons or organisations depends on whether they can control, free of competitive pressure, the use in production of such scarce resources.

The other change affecting the ideas expressed by classical economists has been the enormous increase in the availability of land and natural resources following the colonisation of new lands from the eighteenth century onwards. Land and other natural resources became so abundant that the capacity of their proprietors to extract rent-like payments from their users was closely restricted. Indeed governments, whether imperially based in European capitals or representing the active entrepreneurial classes in the colonised lands themselves, were anxious to press these resources into use. Land was given away, sold or leased for negligible returns, and the royalties demanded by governments, for access to or use of water, forests, minerals and other natural resources, rarely covered the administrative costs of the departments and agencies concerned. This profligate dispersal of the common wealth has continued. A calculation in 1979 of the rentals charged to pastoralists in the Northern Territory for all the land held under granting leases, capitalised at then current rates of interest, suggests a total value for the land concerned of about $2,000,000 – a sum which, even in the current depressed market, would be hard-pressed to buy more than one or two of the more extensive properties concerned.

Because of this apparent abundance of natural resources the most important property rights now are not those with which the classical economists were concerned. Rather they arise, by the arrangements of society, in the widely varying forms of assets – physical, intellectual, legal, political and conventional – which proliferate around the marketplaces of industrial and commercial society. Unlike land in Victorian England they have tended to be held not by a distinct and recognisable class of people but by the fortunate, talented, skilful or the powerful among all classes; by capitalists and entrepreneurs, but also among the providers of professional services and the more fortunate clerical and industrial workers. The similarity of these property rights to those in land has been less easy to recognise and they have, therefore, not often occasioned the social criticism which previously had been directed at the receipts of the non-active landlord. This freedom from criticism has not been enjoyed by those industrial workers in key positions, who have been able to extract a rent-like element in their wages by threat to withhold their services.

In the years before 1973, there was little controversy about the rewards to owners of scarce resources. Land and related natural resources were widely believed to be almost inexhaustible. Those fortunate enough to have property in some other especially favourable resource or capacity generally received its rent-like reward as a component of profit, or of personal wage or salary where it frequently was seen as a just recompense for differential capacity. Oil price rises in 1973 were therefore a sharp and unexpected reminder that the individual who 'possesses exclusive power over some natural agent . . . can claim a share of the produce as a price of consent to its use in production' and that this claim is one 'which cannot be prevented from existing' (J.S. Mill, 1848, 1852).

The sharp rise in crude oil price was a reminder that the claim had to be met, not merely by those who purchased the crude oil itself, but also by all those using it directly or indirectly as a raw material or a source of power in the production of an astonishingly wide range of final consumer goods. The whole of the benefit of the crude oil price rise did not accrue to the owners of the basic resource itself. The comprehensive processes of exploration, development, refining and marketing have been and are performed for these owners usually by a small number of transnational companies. While it is difficult to determine the balance

25

of their respective shares it seems certain that the original rentiers, being those in whose lands or territories the oil wells exist, have had to share the accretion to their rent with these other monopolistically organised capitalists and entrepreneurs.

Between them, however, they would share the benefits of a tremendous, newly recognised source of wealth and a claim on the yield of all forms of production in which their scarce resource was embodied as raw material or energy. Unless offset by other changes these claims would have to be met by reductions in the shares of the yield of productive processes going to those providing the other components involved in it. In other words a consequence of increasing scarcity will almost certainly be a widespread and significant redistribution of wealth and income.

Of course other things will not remain unchanged. Efforts will be made to extend the known reserves of the scarce resource by exploration or improved technology, and alternatives deriving from different basic resources will be pressed into use where comparative prices permit. The composition of the final demand for the whole range of products concerned will be affected by the rise in their prices. The tendency for productivity to rise in other forms of production can be expected to continue. The precise outcome will reflect the combination of technological and demand factors. However, for a material such as oil, now basic to our industrial way of life, it is improbable that elasticities of demand will permit any substantial check to the redistribution of income in favour of the proprietors, brought about by the initial price response to scarcity.

At the level of final demand the social effect of this redistribution will depend upon:

- the level of incomes of those who provide that demand;
- the importance of the final products concerned for the health and welfare of those using them; and
- the capacity of those whose real income is reduced to restore it closer to its original level.

On all three counts it will be the poorest consumers who will suffer most. Studies in the United Kingdom of the effect of increased power

26

and heating charges following the rise in oil price showed severe impact on the aged, the sick and the unemployed. For them heating was particularly critical to reasonable health and comfort, and they lacked the margin of income, the reserves, the knowledge or the bargaining power to respond constructively to the price rise. Such individuals are, however, predominantly outside the productive system and their incomes largely dependent upon statutory or charitable transfers from those more fortunate. Apart from those directly affected in this way, we must follow through the effects of scarcity via increased prices on the rewards flowing to the various factors of production: to the entrepreneur, to the investor who provides the capital for the entrepreneur's venture and to the various categories of labour employed within it or providing services to it and deriving income from it. It is changes in the incomes of persons and corporations which will determine social consequences, but such incomes will be derived from rewards based on their role or roles as factors in production.

It is useful to start with the entrepreneurs – those business people from whose decisions to continue or initiate production the motive power of the economic system derives. Apart from those entrepreneurs (usually transnational corporations) closely involved with the proprietors of oil, and therefore sharing in their rent income, most businesses will have found their level of profit encroached upon by the increases in costs resulting from higher oil prices, especially as the real incomes of their customers will have probably been reduced by rises in the prices of other final consumer goods also affected by these rising costs. Some businesses might, as a result of some monopoly advantage, be able to absorb these reductions and continue to obtain acceptable returns. They are likely, none the less, to struggle to recover their previous rate of return.

Those enterprises closer to the margin, where competition will tend to limit their earnings to the minimum necessary to reward their entrepreneurial effort and cover their risks, may be threatened with having to close down. The ability to avoid this will depend upon each enterprise's capacity:

- to increase the efficiency with which it can use the capital and labour involved by improving technology or organisation;

27

- to extract a greater return from any monopoly element involved in the business; and
- to obtain the capital and labour the enterprise requires at lower cost.

Therefore, following widespread cost increases reflecting shortages in the supply of basic resources, there will be a fiercely competitive scramble among businesses each trying to shift the burden of cost increases on to incomes other than their own. In this task, however, other consequences of the shortages will present them with added problems.

It is characteristic of limited resources that as scarcity becomes more apparent producers are forced to exploit less and less suitable and accessible sources. Thus it has been remarked: 'Every barrel of oil taken out of the ground makes the next barrel more costly' (Commoner, 1975: 212). Certainly the expected capital cost per barrel of oil and gas from the North-west shelf, for instance, is extremely high compared with that of the Bass Strait field. This rising need to extract the increasingly scarce resources will require capital at a time when there is a similar pressure on the demand for capital for other purposes. This pressure is apparent following developments in technology affecting industry and commerce generally – such as computerisation in clerical and industry-servicing occupations. So dominant has been this increasing need for capital that economists and business people in the United States of America and in Australia have for years been talking of a crisis in the supply of capital and urged special measures to give preferential tax treatment to assist enterprises to accumulate funds to meet their own capital needs. To some extent this pressure on the supply of capital can be mitigated if general economic growth is restricted, leaving resource industries with easier access. The increased rent component in the rewards of their proprietors provides some addition to their capacity to provide their own capital, but it will be only in conditions of sharply rising productivity that these factors could offset the basic pressure on the supply of capital over a significant period of time.

Those in a sufficiently strong monopoly position have been able to meet their capital needs by adopting a price policy which extracts from the consumer some of the capital needed. This device not merely contributes to solving the problem of capital supply but also transfers ownership of the capital so accumulated from the consumer who supplied it to the owners of the enterprise. Apart from those so privileged, entrepreneurs face a double squeeze on their profit incomes: with proprietors of scarce resources in a position to extract an increased rent-type income from them and the proprietors of capital generally in a similarly strong position. Entrepreneurs' capacity to restore their profit incomes to conventionally accepted levels will turn, therefore, on their capacity to achieve very high rates of increase in productivity or to force down the level of real wages earned by the different categories of labour.

Increasing productivity, to the extent that it is expressed in the rising output of goods embodying scarce resources, could intensify the problem of scarcity of those resources and, to the extent that it is achieved by lower use of labour per unit of output, will weaken the bargaining power of labour while improving the earnings of the entrepreneur. It is unlikely, therefore, to protect the earnings of labour or significantly alter the employers' desire to reduce them.

In a purely competitive system such a reduction would be brought about by market forces. The increasing cost of scarce natural resources will tend to reduce the productivity of labour, while the tendency of current technological change to lead to the replacement of labour by capital will weaken further the bargaining power of the labour concerned. But the market for labour is not wholly competitive and labour is not a single uniform factor in production. Market forces are constrained by collective bargaining and by institutional procedures for wage determination which will check, but not wholly prevent, the downward pressure on real wages. Furthermore, while technological change makes the bargaining power of labour generally weaker, it places significant competitive strength in the hands of specialist workers upon whom large and complex productive systems depend. This dependence may derive from their specialised knowledge or skills but may come simply from their capacity to withdraw or threaten to withdraw services upon which the whole system depends.

However, such constraints upon the operation of competitive factors in the labour market are likely to slow down rather than prevent the

29

rewards of labour adjusting to its weaker bargaining position. This is the more likely since the decline in the profitability of enterprises other than those extracting natural resources will almost certainly be reflected in low levels of business activity and high levels of unemployment, which will reduce still further the capacity of wage earners to protect their real incomes.

This weakened bargaining power of labour could, wholly or in part, be offset by increasing productivity, yielding a higher total income per capita, of which labour may be able to demand a share. Compared with the recent past, this source seems likely to be less fruitful. Growing resource scarcity is a negative factor in measured productivity and the switch to more capital-intensive and more costly processes will work in the same direction. The productivity of capital will tend to be reduced by both changes. In any event, the need to restore the entrepreneurs' return to a conventionally acceptable level will, at least for some time, take priority over the demands of labour. Particularly since, until that return has been so restored, business activity is likely to remain depressed and labour bargaining power with it. This priority will not be readily conceded by organised labour, especially in those privileged categories which also enjoy some monopoly power. The period of adjustment is likely to be one of industrial unrest although action would probably be confined to such privileged categories.

Thus, simplified economic analysis and a hurried look at commercial experience following the emergence of scarcity in the supplies of crude oil suggest that increasing scarcity of non-renewable resources is likely to lead to:

- a redistribution of wealth in favour of those who own the remainder of those resources, and to increasing rent-type incomes for these proprietors;
- the employment of increasingly costly methods of exploration, extraction and treatment of the scarce resources and the use of more expensive and less technically efficient alternatives. This, together with other technological changes, will place pressure on the supply of capital and tend to increase the share of total production which goes to those who supply that capital;

- a double squeeze from these two sources on the earnings of those who organise production, leading to reduced levels of activity until the conventionally expected levels of entrepreneurial rewards are restored;
- a serious weakening in the bargaining power of labour (except for those who can command a significant monopoly component in their contribution to the productive processes), leading to declining levels of real wages at least until entrepreneurial profits have been restored; and
- a reduced prospect for increasing productivity to which we might otherwise look to counter this decline in real wages.

In brief, increasing scarcity of non-renewable resources will mean, both in terms of wealth and of income, that most of the rich will grow richer and almost all the poor, poorer.

If in fact the oil crisis of the early 1970s was not an isolated event but the beginning of an era of increasing scarcity in non-renewable resources, the consequences I have described will not be a once-for-all adjustment but a continuing process. That crisis could prove to be merely the first of many in which oil prices escalate and oil scarcity is followed by a widening range of scarcities of non-renewable resources. The consequences would thus become continuing characteristics of our economic system within which individual, corporate and political aspirations would be constrained. If I have judged their nature correctly, these consequences will inevitably call into question the presumption which underlies most social and political planning in the western world, at least in industrialised countries – that employment for wages, supplemented by social service benefits for the really poor and the unemployed, can provide the source of rising living standards and an improving quality of life for almost all.

It is important to emphasise that the consequences of increasing scarcity which I have predicated will not have to await the 'doomsday' catastrophes which members of the Club of Rome (a private study group financed largely by wealthy industrialists) and others have foretold. These consequences are indeed aspects of the adjustments which the market mechanism will induce, and is currently inducing, in the process of avoiding or deferring such catastrophes. Are there policies which could mitigate the distributional effects of increasing scarcity and preserve the hope that we can build a society in which wealth and incomes progressively become less rather than more unequal, and in which a lifestyle of good quality is open even to the poorest? There are, of course, those who see in the allocations which result from the workings of the market the expression of divine wisdom or the inevitability of fate and who believe, therefore, that policy should always accord with that wisdom and be directed to expediting a reduction in real wages. There are some aspects of contemporary economic policies which appear to be consciously directed to this end.

Most economists pin their faith on increasing productivity based upon a continuance of recent rates of technological progress and point to the fact that real wages, at least in industrial societies, have risen over past decades. But unless productivity *per unit of natural resources* used, as well as productivity per unit of labour, can be dramatically improved, it is likely that the problems of scarcity of these resources will increase. There is, of course, considerable scope for technology to reduce the quantity of materials used in particular industries. The development of miniaturisation in the electronics industries is an illustration of such an opportunity successfully seized. Many of the ideas put forward by advocates of 'The Conserver Society' (see Science Council of Canada, 1979) are concerned to redirect technology to this and related ends.

It is perhaps salutary to recall that the last great fuel crisis occurred in the fifteenth and sixteenth centuries when disappearing supplies of timber combined with rising population forced the substitution of coal for wood in domestic and industrial use. For many years this substitution involved higher cost and less appropriate technology and its social effects were adverse. It is true that ultimately coal proved to be a remarkably valuable resource and provided a stimulus to technological progress, and these factors in due course made possible the technological dominance of British coal-based industry. But it was many decades before this became evident and perhaps two centuries before the superiority of the new technology was fully demonstrated. For decades the need to resort to coal, for poorer people in particular, would have been seen as reducing their real income and indeed as being the cause of poverty and hardship.

Today technological change is more rapid and more consciously directed, and some economists are confident that it can be counted upon to ensure a level of total output rising fast enough to cover the increasing shares of proprietors of natural resources, and a sufficient surplus for increasing real wages. Attempts to quantify the rate of technological change appear to be of doubtful validity. A belief that the outcome of technological change will invariably be favourable, even when it is initiated by adverse factors such as scarcity, is based upon faith rather than upon either logic or indisputable evidence. Even if such a faith will be justified in the long run, the transition could be traumatic for many and possibly destructive for our society.

More particularly I doubt whether, in the context of increasing scarcity and rising rents to proprietors, labour would in fact tend to benefit from rising productivity. The increases in real wages of recent decades have been achieved in a sellers' market for labour and an expanding market for the products of industry. In a situation where scarcities inhibit improved productivity, where total demand grows more slowly and where technological change tends to displace labour, the bargaining power of most wage earners will prove much less favourable.

I believe it is necessary, therefore, to consider conscious intervention to offset the effects of scarcity on those with low incomes. I do not think such intervention impossible. Scarcity creates the opportunity for an increasing 'unearned increment' to be extracted by proprietors. It would not be technically difficult to ensure that a substantial part of that increment accrues to the community generally.

J.S. Mill pointed out that ownership of scarce natural resources constitutes a monopoly which cannot be prevented from existing. He also adds, in passing, that the monopoly and, therefore, the rent derived from it can be held as a trust for the community. It may be possible, therefore, by holding natural resources as such a trust, to offset, to some extent at least, the adverse effects of scarcity on the distribution of wealth and income without impairing the effectiveness of the economic system, since the proprietor of such resources is essentially passive.

33

In Australian society all natural resources – land, forests, water and minerals – have belonged originally, at least since 1788, to the Crown; that is, to the community generally. Many resources most showing signs of increasing scarcity still so belong. In some instances a charge for access to and use of these resources has been made in the form of a royalty. In their mad rush to exploit these resources, our rulers have recklessly given them away, sold them for a pittance or made them available for nominal royalties to entrepreneurs who have used them for their own profit. In other words, the benefit which ownership of them confers has been taken from the community and given or sold cheaply to private interests. While the resources concerned were relatively plentiful, this has perhaps been of little significance. But as they become increasingly scarce, the rent that all but the poorest of them can command will continue to rise, and the transfer of community income to individual or corporate proprietors will grow correspondingly. Even where more substantial royalties have been charged, or where they have been supplemented by special tax measures, these measures have not been designed to direct the surplus derived from the special characteristics of the resources concerned to the community, their proper owner.

A tax on resources already alienated from the Crown, if it is to return to the community the potential rent inherent in its ownership, must be flexible in its incidence so that it increases as profits (including that rent) rise with increasing scarcity. It may not be easy to design such taxes. However, I would like to draw attention to a proposal put forward by a negotiator for the Aborigines of the Alligator River region, Northern Territory, in connection with the plans to mine uranium. The proposal appeared capable of directing, for Aboriginal benefit, an important part of the rent which could accrue to the owners of the uranium ore in that region (Stephen Zorn, pers. comm.).

Briefly, the proposal was that the Aboriginal communities should receive a basic royalty, calculated as a percentage of the value of the ore mined, and a share of earnings if they exceeded a standard return on capital, determined by a formula. The formula by which this standard was to be fixed would have enabled the mining operator to meet all running costs and the costs of capital expenditure incurred in the year concerned, and to service capital used in the project, both equity and borrowed, at a rate corresponding to the current rate of interest for debenture capital. Clearly, this formula regarded earnings in excess of these components as being composed substantially of the rent arising from the monopoly involved in ownership of the uranium ore.

I believe this proposal contains the essential elements of a resources tax designed to restore to the community a major part of the rent income derived from the resources which properly belong to it. Only if such a tax falls more heavily on that part of income earned from the use of scarce resources which exceeds the minimum return to the capital involved or required to bring the resources into use, will it adequately acknowledge the rent-like character of that income and protect the community's proprietary rights in it. Such a resource tax should, in my view, be imposed on all enterprises to which access and use of publicly owned resources has been granted. It is perhaps unnecessary to say that the government rejected the proposal, preferring to adhere to a fixed royalty on the value of ore mined and indeed to give away its right to impose special taxes on the project's profits. Such a preference placed the interests of the companies concerned ahead of those of the Aboriginal people involved and the Australian community generally.

The mere existence of such a tax would be insufficient to counter fully the effects on the distribution of wealth and income which will flow from increasing scarcity. If the proceeds of such taxes continue, like present royalties, to be paid into Consolidated Revenue and used for government expenditure in general, they are, in effect, being distributed to members of the community proportionately to the amount of tax those members pay; in other words, in a way which adds to, rather than reduces, income inequality. If income derived from ownership of property which belongs to the community as a whole is to provide a counter to the impoverishment of the poor, it should be distributed at least uniformly through the community. The need for such a counter may become the more urgent as scarcities add to the impoverishment and reduce the bargaining power of wage earners.

It is, of course, not only the proceeds of royalties and similar Crown income from community property which, by being paid direct to revenue and used to finance expenditure, intensifies existing inequalities.

35

The community is also the proprietor of a number of enterprises, including banks and airlines. These activities, together with the increasing potential for rent income of publicly owned resources, create the possibility of all personal incomes including a significant rentier component.

Indeed, it is a favourite dream of mine that there might be established a National Estate which, administered by trustees for the community, would be the proprietor of:

- the National Estate in the sense of those things like national parks, historic buildings, works of art which we 'want to keep' and which are a source of current enjoyment and important components in the quality of life;
- the natural resources belonging to the community as a whole – Crown land, water, state forests and minerals; and
- the income-earning assets owned by governments and public authorities on behalf of the community.

To these assets might be added the proceeds of estate and death duties paid, perhaps, in bonds and shares and other assets at current valuations which could steadily increase the community's share of total wealth and the income derived from it.

It would be the responsibility of those administering this Estate to protect and improve its capacity to contribute directly to the quality of life; to husband its scarce resources with reasonable concern for the future; to ensure to the community the rent which could be derived from them; and to use its income partly to provide public facilities and services and to distribute the balance equally to all members of the community.

In a community in which such an institution existed, one could envisage a steadily increasing proportion of individual incomes being derived from access to public goods and services available to all or from rentier-type receipts from the National Estate. The steady increase in this proportion could prove a less disruptive way of achieving greater equality of income and of establishing a floor under the incomes of the poor, than those on which we now rely. Indeed one may well doubt whether, in a system where many people own no productive assets outside their own persons and where income from jobs is the main instrument of distribution, any significant improvement in the equality of incomes is likely to be achieved. Incidentally, any rentier receipts which can be added to the incomes of potential wage earners would also strengthen the independence and bargaining power of those who otherwise would depend for their security upon the outcome of industrial bargaining from a position of economic weakness.

These ideas may be the stuff from which only pipe-dreams are made, but unless we can find ways (to quote J.S. Mill) '. . . of holding scarce resources in trust for the community generally', the market response to scarcities is likely to produce results incompatible with the best social aspirations of our society.

The picture I have painted of the economic effects of increasing scarcity is, I agree, pessimistic – indeed dismal – and the ideas I have canvassed for preventing those effects from destroying our aspirations for a more just and humane society are visionary – perhaps fanciful. Nevertheless, I find the pessimism inescapable, and I am sure that only boldness and ingenuity of imagination can enable equity and compassion genuinely to become the hallmarks of our social and economic institutions.

I see no escape from increasing scarcity or from the difficulties this will create for the continuance of a pattern of life whose quality is judged by the quantity of goods produced and whose value is thought to be increased by the reckless dissipation of our patrimony of resources. As I have argued elsewhere (see Chapter 7), the factors which determine the quality of life are in fact derived much more from the environment in which people's activities are carried out, and from the degree to which those activities provide them with a sense of worthwhile purpose and a healthy balance of security and challenge, of companionship and privacy, of belonging and of individuality. There are even now in different parts of the world and in our own society men and women who live healthy, vigorous, exciting and dignified lives on incomes, and with access to resources, that seem pitiably small to us.

I believe we can, without monastic austerity, design lifestyles at least as healthful, stimulating and satisfying as those we now lead, with markedly less dependence on the goods and processes of the market-place than at present and with much smaller risks of disruptive scar-cities. Work in Canada reported by the Canadian Science Council (1979) has explored a wide range of modifications of contemporary consumption patterns which would contribute to such lifestyles. These modifications will require ingenuity and imagination if they are to be achieved and would be stimulated by changes in our personal and social values. It is, I believe, time we began to exercise such ingenuity and to cultivate such values.

3

Matching Ecological and Economic Realities

Introductory lecture to symposium on 'Environmental Quality and Resource Management: Political, Legal and Administrative Realities', Twelfth Pacific Science Congress, Canberra, August 1971. Published in The Journal *of the Economic Society of Australia and New Zealand, 1972.*

IN a recent lecture entitled 'Man's Place in Nature' Professor R.O. Slatyer (1970) of the Australian National University outlined what he believed to be the main requirements for ecological stability and long-term human survival – which he summed up as 'living ecologically'. There was no doubt in Slatyer's mind that it was possible for humankind to live ecologically, but he commented that to attempt it 'in the short run probably makes economic nonsense'. This comment sounds odd to economists who have always believed that being economic meant making the best use of limited resources, an object which seems closely allied to that for which ecologists plead. Indeed, Professor Lionel Robbins (1932), a distinguished economist and teacher, once defined economics as 'the science which studies human behaviour as a relationship between ends and scarce means which have alternative uses'. Perhaps what Professor Slatyer means is that for humankind to live ecologically would be unwelcome to those who make profits from helping it to live unecologically; or possibly that those now living would be called on to make unwelcome sacrifices in the interests of future generations. In any case the use of scarce resources is involved in the issues with which Professor Slatyer was concerned and, therefore, they can be looked at in economic terms.

39

If it is true that humanity's long-term welfare – and perhaps survival – is threatened by the use we make of the resources made available by the natural system of which we are part, then this should be a problem of deep concern to economists. This is the more so since those who most vehemently criticise human behaviour in this matter see as a major defect in this behaviour an excessive valuation of economic growth, a quality of contemporary life to which economists have devoted much attention and from which, many have argued, humankind derives significant benefit. This criticism has been graphically expressed by my friend Professor W.E.H. Stanner who sees the contemporary worship of economic growth as a sophisticated form of the cargo cults of the non-literate societies with which he was concerned. These cults are marked by an overvaluation of cargo as an embodiment and symbol of wealth and power. 'All such cults', he comments, 'have their priests and theologians and the economist, with his glorification of output and consumption and the mystic symbols by which he purports to measure them, has assumed their mantle. God is goods, and the GNP the outward and visible sign of his glory and his power!'

If this charge can be laid against the contemporary economist it is because he has been seduced into heresy. The optimum use of scarce resources has always been the basic concern of the discipline. It was also an economist, Malthus, who first (almost 200 years ago) drew attention to the potential conflict of rising populations with limited resources – and fundamentally for the same reasons given by contemporary critics. Indeed, if one wished to be captious one could point out that it was not the economists who ignored the impact of scientific discovery on birth and survival rates as increasing the threat of 'famine, pestilence and war' as the only effective means to population control, or who held out visions of a future in which science and technology would solve all problems and open up limitless vistas of universal affluence.

Perhaps there is nothing to be gained by interdisciplinary recriminations. But it is sometimes necessary for all disciplines to question their conscious and unconscious assumptions and the contemporary relevance of analysis developed in radically different situations. It is wise to recall Huxley's dictum: 'It is the fate of new truths to begin as heresies

40

and to end as superstitions'. Economists should be prepared to consider how far the new truths about the importance of output which began as heresies in the 1930s may have become superstitions, making greater the threat of permanent ecological damage. The risk that this damage will cumulatively endanger the human species is, I believe, none the less real because it is sometimes urged upon us extravagantly and with apparent masochistic pleasure in our impending doom. Therefore I propose to accept broadly the need for humanity to 'live ecologically' and to consider rather some of the economic and organisational problems which will confront us in trying to do so.

In particular I will look at the following broad questions:

- What would be the economic characteristics of an ecologically acceptable system?
- What institutional changes would such a system call for?
- Must it be a non-growth system?
- Would it permit improvements in the standard and quality of life?
- Would such a system provide a pattern of life capable of meeting the biological needs of the human species?

THE ECONOMIC CHARACTERISTICS OF AN ECOLOGICALLY ACCEPTABLE ECONOMIC SYSTEM

Briefly, the ecologist sees humanity threatened by the effects of an exponentially growing population pressing on an environment which is finite. Population growth and increased production and consumption of commodities, stimulated by capital investment, put exponentially increasing pressure on resources, some of which are already in sight of depletion, and threaten with pollution the natural environment not merely of ourselves but also of species on which we are dependent in ways and to degrees we do not fully understand.

About the form of the resultant catastrophe ecologists are less precise. Population is seen first growing beyond the capacity of its finite environment, being halted by whatever proves to be the contemporary equivalent of Malthus's 'famine, pestilence or war' (Malthus, 1798, *Essay on the Principle of Population*); and then in the consequence falling perhaps far below the point of equilibrium.

The ecologist doubts whether the world population will pass successfully through those fluctuations of reducing amplitude tending towards equilibrium which are characteristic of the populations of other creatures which from time to time suffer population explosions. Humanity is a long-lived creature with an extended childhood during which its full potential demand on resources is hidden. The excess of numbers will be with us before we are fully aware of the danger. As Plutarch (fourth and fifth centuries AD) said: 'We are more sensible of what is done against custom than against nature'. Furthermore, our occupancy of the environment is or threatens to be so complete, our effect on its resources and character so destructive, the possibilities of genetic damage to our own species so real, that the extinction of the human race – perhaps of all forms of life – cannot wholly be discounted, especially if the conflicts of interest provoked by competition for critical resources lead to the lunacy of atomic war.

The most sophisticated expositions of this thesis are the most pessimistic. They emphasise that economic processes form a system and that the causally operating factors in that system are mutually interrelated, with significant feedbacks. An attempt to limit one of the causes of potential disaster is likely merely to create conditions in which the others will prove even more destructive. It is not sufficient to tinker: we must comprehend the effect of what we do on the system as a whole with the fullest understanding and recognition of its complex relationships and feedbacks.

Without detailed knowledge of the assumptions about the nature of the relationships on which these expositions are based one cannot assess their validity, but I feel intuitively that they probably assume too great a constancy in people's values and consequently in the demands they make on the system. They also underestimate changes in relationships which would flow from alterations in these values and demands and consequently their effect on the system.

In essence the ecologist's prescription for this malaise, however difficult to act upon, is clear. We must:

- halt the growth of world population, reduce it at least in some regions (perhaps particularly in populous and technically sophisticated cities) and stabilise it at an ecologically safe level;
- limit the use of scarce resources and ideally use only those which are capable of perpetual production or perfect recycling;
- use our resources only in ways which do not threaten the survival of other living species;
- control, to a level of safety within the absorptive capacity of the environment, the emission of waste products, particularly those of a kind or those produced on a scale likely to affect the ecological balance, such as heat from the use of energy and waste from nuclear energy generation.

I am not competent to judge how absolutely or with what speed it will be necessary for the world to conform with this prescription – nor to judge how far, if at all, increasing knowledge will enable us to postpone or avoid the need to conform.

The urge to seek such postponements opens up a fascinating field of speculation about what will happen once the implications of the finite environment are fully recognised. One can imagine convulsive redistributions of people and the emergence of a desperate technology for the arid, the wet, cold and inhospitable lands, for the sea floor and perhaps for the moon: the last frantic flowering of the technological civilisation.

But judgements about how quickly or absolutely we must accept the ecologist's prescription are not necessary for my present purposes. Provided we believe that people must live more ecologically and that to do so will involve substantial changes in their behaviour, we can with advantage consider the economic and organisational problems such changes will present and the impact they will have on the nature of society itself.

Let me turn now to the economic character of a system which would more nearly meet the ecologist's prescription and consider what the economist's skills can contribute to its realisation. In seeking an answer to this question one must differentiate between what might happen in the transition to an ecologically acceptable economy and what is likely when it has been established as a going concern.

43

Economically the outstanding features of the present non-ecological situation are:

- that mankind is living to a significant degree on a heritage of non-replaceable resources;
- that producers of many products are obtaining these resources, and others for whose replacement or recycling special measures are necessary, at prices which do not ensure equilibrium between the long-term demand for and supply of them; and
- that some forms of production involve costs of a kind which fall on persons other than those producing or consuming the goods concerned. Such social costs are rarely charged against the producer or consumer.

It is probably simplest to see all three aspects of the present system as problems of the relative prices of the goods and resources concerned. Economists, partly for the sake of simplicity, regard the various factors of production as in essence substitutable. This assumption is not wholly misleading. A product which can be produced with one mix of resources (capital, labour, materials, skill and entrepreneurial capacity) can also be produced (at different cost) with other possible mixes. In other words, if the use of some resources was prohibited or controlled to guarantee their conservation, effective replacement or recycling, it would generally still be technically possible to produce goods serving the same purposes but they would almost certainly cost more. If resources important to human survival are being used recklessly, if goods are being produced in ways which produce harmful side-effects, then the logical behaviour from an economist's point of view would be to increase the prices of the resources concerned or the offending process until their use was brought effectively under control. In some cases the price would have to be high enough effectively to prohibit the use of the resources or process concerned.

The immediate effect, therefore, of economic measures to restrain 'non-ecological' tendencies in our present system would be to bring about a sharp rise in the prices of many classes of goods. Assuming constant incomes and no change in the pattern of consumers' preferences, this would mean a fall in the standard of living of those who used them.

44

The full effect would be complex. Firstly, for those resources which were privately owned, changes in relative prices and the effects of replacement or recycling requirements would bring about changes in the pattern of accumulated wealth. Changes in relative prices would require drastic changes in the pattern of production to meet the new order of consumers' preferences at current prices. These changes would themselves stimulate technological changes and shifts in the profitability of enterprises – perhaps in the relative affluence of different communities.

But it cannot be assumed that demand would change only because of alterations in relative prices – the effects of the decision to 'live ecologically' could profoundly alter the balance of people's preferences. Goods now regarded as symbols of affluence and of status may become socially proscribed and the pattern of life may be so altered as to call for new types of economic effort and enterprise to meet its needs.

The contraction of the use of material resources for the production of commodities is likely to free human resources for other purposes. It would be possible to employ some of these in an enrichment of the physical environment, in providing wider and more readily available services, and the means to a more richly endowed leisure. Above all, at no personal cost there would be, for all, the benefit from the decline of the '*dis*amenities' of pollution and from the recovery of the natural environment.

The balance between these conflicting consequences cannot confidently be foreseen. It would appear practically certain that if society's wants and relative valuations remained unchanged the transition to an ecologically oriented economy would involve a sharp reduction in standards of living. But wants and values are in no sense absolute. They would be affected by the processes involved in the change itself and must, to some extent, be presumed to be different in reflection of the collective decision to make the change.

INSTITUTIONAL CONSEQUENCES AND PROBLEMS

Looked at in terms of elementary economic analysis, it is easy enough to see the transition to an ecologically acceptable economic system as essentially one of adapting the pattern of prices so that long-term equilibrium is achieved between the demand for and supply of scarce resources. But it is obvious that the present institutional pattern of our economic system is not going to produce such an adaptation. It is worthwhile, therefore, to speculate on the nature and probability of the changes which might be necessary to achieve it.

The first and perhaps most difficult problem concerns the time horizon within which people make their decisions. It is not enough for humanity to be convinced that it is collectively wasting a heritage of irreplaceable resources and despoiling an environment to the damage of future generations. It must also be prepared to take the welfare of such generations effectively in the calculus by which decisions are made. People find it hard to give their own future needs and those of their immediate families an importance equal to that they attach to the gratification of present needs or desires. How much more reluctantly will they forgo such gratifications in the interests of generations unborn, for the bulk of whom they can have no imaginable sense of personal concern?

It is true that people have a capacity to identify themselves with corporate institutions, with 'perpetual succession' and to make decisions for welfare beyond the limits of their own lifetime and which can involve sacrifice of immediate satisfactions. Members of a club, alumni of a university, devotees of a religion, members of racial groups, of political parties, indeed of communities and nations themselves – all at some times, for some purposes and to some degree, exhibit this willingness to subordinate their individual welfare to that of group effectiveness, welfare and survival. In most of these instances, however, there is an element of exclusiveness in the identification – a tendency to see the particular group as distinct from, and perhaps even opposed to or threatened by, the wider categories of those 'without the law'. Will it be possible to extend the range and comprehensiveness of such loyalties so that they comprehend a concern for the human species now and for ever?

Such an extension seems incompatible with the emphasis which Australian civilisation – for the last 200 years at least – has placed upon the value of the individual. In an ecological world we are likely to become more community-minded, with the scope of the community and the

46

closeness of its integration being progressively strengthened – perhaps until Marshall McLuhan's image of the 'global village' is realised. The individual in such a society will be a strangely different creature.

But let us glance at the institutional changes of a more immediate and practical character which may be necessary to promote a more ecologically oriented pattern of life – especially in respect of population, exhaustible resources and pollution.

So far as population is concerned, medical science and social welfare policies have almost eliminated the natural checks on pregnancies and births and have so extended the allotted span of individual life that the relative stability once characteristic of human communities has been destroyed. While it is true that some sophisticated urban societies seem, by a variety of means, to have restored this balance, in most places pregnancies and births exceed not merely those necessary to maintain the population but also those which would deliberately be chosen by the parents. Effective limitation is prevented partly by economic difficulties but perhaps mainly by ignorance, apathy and the strength of conflicting social and religious attitudes.

Programs to make effective free choice about pregnancy and childbirths, backed by education, subsidised equipment and materials, would almost certainly check the growth of population, but whether they would bring it within the ecologist's prescription is uncertain. Ultimately, short of compulsory sterilisation, the determining factor will be the 'platonic idea' of the desired family which people bear in their minds. Who can say what will determine that? It seems in our society to have gone through some surprisingly radical changes during my own lifetime.

Scarce resources can be economised to whatever degree is thought desirable by the effective use of the price mechanism. There is certain to be resistance to dramatic increases in prices which would be seen as threatening accepted standards. Furthermore, where resources and the industries using them are privately owned, increased prices limiting their use are unlikely to be imposed voluntarily. However, if the community could be convinced that effective control was essential, the task would not be impossible. Many of the critical resources – oil, coal, minerals – are in most societies already the property of the State, and

47

others could presumably be made so by legislative act and the terms of their use legislatively controlled. Compensation to private owners of property may be necessary to cover the loss of 'legitimate expectations', and it is possible to see these being balanced by a series of 'betterment taxes' on those whose assets would have appreciated in value. The complexity of such measures appals but they are not impossible.

A possible institutional structure would be a legislatively established 'Scarce Resources Corporation' in which were vested, for the purpose of conservation, all supplies of specified resources, known and as yet unknown. If such a corporation were required within a specified period to bring the use of a particular material to a long-term equilibrium or a particularly specified level, the corporation could give notice of progressively rising prices over that period, thus giving producers time to test alternatives and to develop effective reproductive or recycling techniques.

An alternative to the determination of 'long-term equilibrium' prices by the 'Scarce Resources Corporation' in accordance with its legislative charter would be the imposition of excise taxes, where necessary at prohibitive rates, on the use of scarce resources. This alternative would make the determination of effective prices the function of the legislature. One must take leave to doubt the effectiveness of such an alternative. It is possible to conceive a legislature, sufficiently imbued with ecological fervour, and sufficiently pressed by community opinion, deciding that scarce resources must be effectively rationed, establishing an agency for this purpose and, subject to general supervision by the legislature, trusting it to give effect to this purpose. But I find it impossible to conceive a legislature, torn by the desire for competitive political advantage, and under the inevitable pressure to defer the unpleasant, finding certainty and determination enough to impose effectively restrictive taxes by year-to-year budgetary decision.

The control of pollutant-producing processes could present similar difficulties. For these, a publicly responsible corporation with price-fixing powers would not be adequate. It would be necessary to rely on complex regulations involving supervision and the imposition of penalties, or alternatively on excise taxes on the commodities produced by

48

the offending processes, or preferably on the polluting effluents themselves – their measurement being checked by publicly responsible authorities.

A good case can be made for reliance on excise taxes reflecting themselves in higher prices to the community in these instances. They would ensure maximum pressure on, and maximum stimulus to, the producing enterprise to improve its techniques. More generally, controls which are exercised through the price mechanism have a better record of effectiveness. They are flexible, apparently impersonal and, above all, familiar. They do not obviously impose the will of authority on the private or business behaviour of the citizen and, therefore, are less likely to be thought arbitrary and resented accordingly. They avoid, too, the need for continuous justification by moral exhortation – a process to which ecologists are perhaps unduly prone and to which unregenerate 'economic man' is proverbially allergic.

Just as important as these negative measures will be the action necessary to divert resources into ecologically more acceptable goods and services. A decline in the production of industrially produced commodities will free human resources for the production of other desired goods and especially perhaps services. Many see it possible for us to live in gracious cities and towns well endowed with parks and gardens, with schools and universities, with playing fields, museums, art galleries and theatres, with ready access to an unspoilt natural environment rich in beauty and the range of living species which constitute the web of life.

It is characteristic of many of these things, and the services which they provide, that they are wholly or partly public in character. So far as they require production it must be by collective decision, and it is often purposeless or self-defeating to seek to cover their cost by charges in the ordinary way. Some shift of resources between the public and private sectors of expenditure seems an unavoidable consequence of these changes.

Such a shift will not be easy and may well require institutional changes which we might at present find hard to accept. Experience in most democratic countries seems to suggest that it is harder to finance 'public' goods than private. Even when people collectively rate edu-

49

cation highly, it is more difficult to finance schools and universities than television sets and motor-cars. It is easier to finance motor-cars than adequate highways for them to drive on. This affluence in things bought and sold privately, and poverty in those bought and consumed collectively, is characteristic of our industrial, consumer societies and change in it will encounter strong resistance from 'business' interests.

It may become necessary, if public goods are to receive their proper balance, to modify the present system of income distribution so as to reserve to the State part of the gross national product before it is allocated as personal and corporate incomes. If sufficient natural resources remained or became the property of the State as frequently as do minerals and forests, and sufficient royalties and rents were charged for their employment, the income from this 'community estate' might finance many of the public goods and services concerned. Alternatively, we might need to take a leaf from the book of the collectivist societies which usually deduct a substantial percentage from the proceeds of all sales before they are distributed to those concerned with their production and distribution. This device is, of course, no more than a universal sales tax, but without some such device I find it difficult to see how the apparently innate unwillingness of individuals effectively to finance public goods – however highly valued by taxpayers in their more rational moments – can be overcome.

The shifts in the use of resources, the willingness to accept higher prices or qualitative restrictions, the need for pressure for legislative action, and the evolution of new institutions designed to make these effective, are unlikely unless the community generally accepts the ecologist's gospel and develops a pattern of values and demands on the economic system compatible with it. Human values are not immutable and indeed are evident in kaleidoscopic variety among a multitude of societies. A thought for the hectic changes of sartorial fashion in our own society is enough to demonstrate how malleable and in a sense how conformist they are.

There are those who see advertising as the prime reason for our fanatical urge for consumption and for possessions. This view is almost certainly exaggerated but, in a time when a swing away from material goods is called for, a prohibition on advertising or its exclusion from acceptable costs for the purpose of taxation would appear to have attractions.

There are others who see advertising, in these art-starved times, as the genuine popular visual and literary art of our age, ranging from the Cinderella myths of the cosmetic merchants to the op-art of the Kings Cross lights. To these an alternative suggestion might appeal: a law which required each dollar spent in persuasion to purchase to be balanced by a dollar paid to an official agency to be used in persuasion that the commodity concerned can well be done without. Believers in the virtues of competition, as are most good businessmen, also might find this idea attractive. Certainly it should appeal to advertising agencies.

But changes in values are fundamental to the emergence of the ecologically acceptable economic system. One need not wholly despair of such changes. It is, as Keynes (1936) said, ideas, not vested interests, that are dangerous for good or evil. The transformation of public attitudes on questions of conservation and pollution in the last few years is beyond the wildest hopes of the earnest few who pioneered these ideas. But more than the rational and selective advocacy which characterises present attitudes will be necessary. It will be necessary for people to 'internalise', as the psychologists say, this ecological doctrine so that it becomes part of the unconscious motivation which moulds their conscious thoughts and actions. It is interesting to speculate on what manner of individual will achieve such a 'translation'. This is a matter to which I shall return.

Before I do so I want to touch on two questions: whether an ecologically acceptable economy would permit economic growth; and whether anything useful can be said about the comparative standard or quality of life it would permit.

WOULD SUCH AN ECONOMY BE A STATIC OR 'NON-GROWTH' SYSTEM?

Some scientists and economists have argued that an ecologically acceptable economy must be a static-state system – one in which growth in economic terms would no longer be possible. Such a prospect tends to send cold shudders down the spines of economists as well as those of bustling entrepreneurs and all who take pride in the characteristic achievements of industrial civilisation. It is worth our while, therefore, to consider whether growth and ecological living are incompatible.

Growth occurs when from year to year the system produces, or obtains by exchange with other communities, an increasing quantity of goods and services of a kind the community desires. (These goods and services are assumed not to have changed so much in composition as to invalidate comparisons of their total values from year to year.) This growth derives from two sources: firstly from an increase in the resources used (mainly labour and materials), and secondly from an increase in the efficiency with which they are employed.

Economic growth has not been a negligible factor in human welfare. Our industrial society, with all its faults, has offered greater freedom and opportunity to multitudes of people who for the first time have been offered effective access to an enormous range of new experiences, a widely varied choice of occupation and of leisure-time pursuits, as well as possessions of infinite diversity. For many the last few decades have been, and have been felt to be, a time of personal liberation and enhancement.

It is this sense of enjoying the fruits of an affluent system, however materialist and philistine, which influences and may determine the reaction of many (both among the 'plain men' and the economists) to the ecologist's plea. They hear this plea as a *cri du coeur* of a privileged class – a class already well equipped with cars and other material goods, with pleasant homes with views, enjoying the opportunity to travel to unfamiliar and exciting places, and with leisure to enjoy the solitude and enchantment of an unspoilt natural environment. They hear this class pleading with pious sermons on conservation and pollution in a desperate effort to protect itself against the loss of freedom of the roads as more and more of the proletariat drive on them, against the interruption of their views by overhead telephone wires, lopped trees and vulgar blocks of flats as 'select' residential areas are invaded by the *nouveau riche*, and against their personal enjoyment of strange and unfamiliar places, of solitude and natural beauty being violated by the beer cans, the plastic containers and the other impedimenta of mass tourism. Indeed, it could well be that if ecologists wish to be heard the first thing they should do is to sell their cars as an earnest of their sincerity. Sir Harry Pilkington, millionaire director of the Bank of England, always rode to the Bank on a push-bike. His views on the pollution of the city by motor-vehicle exhaust fumes might well be listened to with more respect than most.

Growth, too, has been important to management – management of individual enterprises and of the economy as a whole. Management involves a continuous process of adjustment – to meet changing consumer demands, to take advantage of new technology, to correct for past errors, to redistribute responsibility, to find promotion for the able and ambitious, and to ease out with dignity those who have passed their best. All of these are done more easily, more effectively and with less waste in a situation of growth. The same is true for the economy as a whole. To change the pattern of industry, to redistribute resources, to liquidate the obsolescent – all are easier in a context of growth. The wage-earner, the professional, indeed practically everybody, has become convinced of the boasted illimitable and burgeoning fecundity of the economic system and seeks regular evidences of his or her effective participation in its benefits. Growth makes it possible, to some degree at least, to satisfy their expectations and to avoid in part the gross inflation which their pressures for increased income would otherwise involve.

Above all, growth has been the guarantee that resources – particularly labour – will be as fully employed as it wishes; that there will be a level of investment adequate to employ the resources freed by savings from current consumption; that people generally will be able to use their energy, their intelligence, their training and their experience purposefully and, of course, remuneratively. Whatever may be said for leisure as a component in 'living ecologically', there is little to be said for compulsory and unpaid leisure.

Managers and administrators in a non-growth economy would, therefore, find their tasks more difficult, and the risks of failure would be the greater. But need an ecologically acceptable economy be without

53

growth? In such an economy population would be stable and physical resources previously unknown unlikely. Growth could derive, therefore, only from more effective use of known resources and from the development of new goods and services employing little or no scarce materials. Growth from such sources can be significant. It derives from the more effective use of capital, from increasing knowledge, from improved organisation and from imaginative entrepreneurship – the capacity to recognise and make effective new opportunities to combine resources for human benefit or enjoyment.

With stable (and possibly smaller) populations, many communities will still have high levels of per capita income. The incentives and social organisations which ensure a high level of savings from such incomes will remain. And there seems no reason to doubt that increasing knowledge will continue to develop and that technology, innovation and entrepreneurship will persist. The higher pattern of prices we envisage for those commodities which employ scarce resources or impose social costs on others would not destroy the possibility of profit from their production for a smaller market and might even provide a powerful stimulus to innovation – particularly innovation directed towards a reduction of materials content and the power required for their production. Furthermore, there will be commodities the demand for which is increased by the necessary technical changes. For example, if the need to use power more economically made central heating impossibly expensive, or perhaps a socially prohibited luxury, the increased demand for woollen underwear might transform the prospects of our pastoralists and make them once more the landed aristocracy rather than the mendicant dependants they are in the process of becoming.

Exciting possibilities for entrepreneurship could well emerge from the shifting pattern of demand which could spring from the changing price relationships and (hopefully) from the ecologically oriented valuations which people would need to acquire. Economically speaking there are no necessarily catastrophic revolutions involved in this. Between communities in different parts of the world and between communities in different historical epochs, there are and have been widely differing relative price structures. Given time, an economic system can adjust to these differences.

Essentially, then, a world with a stable population, with ecologically oriented values and with a startlingly different set of relative prices could still have:

- savings representing a significant proportion of total income;
- a growing body of scientific knowledge and technological skills; and
- a fund of organisational and entrepreneurial capacity.

These are the ingredients of growth and I see no reason why, after the transition to an ecologically acceptable economy was complete, they would not continue to provide the stimulus to the production of progressively more of the goods and services demanded or their production at progressively lower real cost.

Indeed, there would be a risk that in some wealthy communities savings would be excessive. Without the need to provide social and productive equipment for increasing numbers each year, the demand for capital would be less. Higher relative prices for industrially produced goods and other restraints on the use of certain materials and processes producing pollutants could reduce some opportunities for investment. Since the incentives for and sources of savings are at least partly independent of the demand for them created by the desire to invest, there could be a need and an opportunity to find additional ways of employing the resources freed by the continuing savings. But when one thinks for a moment of the vast improvements possible in the quality of our physical environment, the need to regenerate our cities, to develop space for outdoor recreation, to house and present the arts, to provide facilities for education, for research and for contemplation, fears that we may run out of worthwhile projects are dissipated like mist in the wind. Furthermore, much of the world will for decades, perhaps for generations, continue to be overpopulated and poorly equipped. The people of these parts of the world will need urgently any resources wealthier countries feel able to spare.

WOULD IMPROVEMENTS IN THE STANDARD AND QUALITY OF LIFE BE POSSIBLE?

Judgements about changes in the standard and quality of life provided by an ecologically acceptable economic system are difficult, if not impossible, to answer objectively. Economists tend to think of and to seek to measure the standard of living of a community as the value of the gross national product divided by the number of people in it. They will perhaps modify this measure according to their prejudices by taking into account the way in which this product is distributed between members of the community. This concept of the gross national product has a specious air of objectivity and, despite its usefulness as a tool of economic management, begs more fundamental questions than it answers. Perhaps because of this there has recently been a tendency to talk of the 'quality of life' as something different and more important. This quality is seen as a measure of the degree to which a society offers effective opportunity to enjoy the 'good life'. The components of the good life are a combination of goods and services available in a total environment, physical, social and cultural, and their precise composition would be a matter of personal judgement about which widely differing opinions would be held. The 'quality of life', therefore, is an essentially subjective concept. It may be, however, that for a particular community a reasonable consensus could be found about the range of choice of goods and services and about the qualities of the environment which should be offered.

Let us see, without thinking too precisely on the event, whether commonsense judgements are possible about the standard and quality of life in an ecologically acceptable system.

Firstly, that part of the standard and quality of life which is provided by material goods and possessions would almost certainly be poorer. Commodities would be fewer and markedly more expensive. To this extent the transition would involve a loss of standards. To some extent this loss may be reduced by the effects of the ecologist's prescription on population, which would need to be stabilised and in many countries reduced. There are certainly some communities where both the standard and the quality of life in the senses I have used these terms could still be improved by an increase in population. For some commodities

56

reasonable economies of scale do not emerge for really small markets. Small communities may offer a restricted range of educational opportunity and occupation, and it is unusual, for instance, for them to provide very generously for participation in or enjoyment of the arts. These instances are, however, the exception rather than the rule. Apart from the qualifications they suggest, it seems certain that income per head could (other things being equal) be higher and the environmental quality better if populations were smaller.

At the level of the individual and the family, judgement becomes more difficult. A community with constant or falling population will have many families with no children or with only one child. Families of more than two would be unusual, and more than three would probably have to be regarded as socially scandalous. Most authorities on child welfare would, I think, argue that the single child often misses out on much, and many psychiatrists would see the childless or one-child family as a frequent source of frustration and emotional deprivation. On the other hand, greater freedom from the demands of motherhood would free the physical, intellectual and emotional capacities of many women for a wider social role. Many of them would welcome this and there can be little doubt that society would be the richer.

The reduction in the quantity of material goods produced would free resources which could be used, for instance, to reduce pollution and to protect other living species. These may add little to the gross national product but would improve the quality of life by reducing many of the *dis*satisfactions which represent the social costs of present forms of production. They would also restore some sources of satisfaction which the industrial society is progressively destroying.

All these considerations arise from the impact of the transition to an ecologically acceptable economy. When all has been allowed for, my guess is that the transition will prove a difficult - indeed traumatic - experience.

Once the transition has been made it would be possible, as I have argued, for the emergent patterns of goods and services demanded to be provided progressively more cheaply and abundantly.

However, any attempt to make quantitative comparisons between our present standards or quality of life and those of an ecologically acceptable system is futile. Such standards are a relationship between what is sought and what the system offers. We have seen that so fundamental a change in purposes will be reflected in society's values and therefore in the demands people make of the system. Furthermore, the radical changes in the composition of the goods and services produced expose in their most extreme form the unreality of the assumptions on which computations of the gross national product and the standard of life are built.

But for mankind to stay alive, it has been said, it must compare as well as count. There are, I believe, certain basic requirements which humankind shares with other species. Ecologists argue that some of these are threatened by the continuance of our present system. It may be possible to speculate about how far they can be met in the alternative.

WOULD A SYSTEM OF THIS KIND MEET HUMAN NEEDS?

It has been said that human beings, as individuals or as communities, need identity, security and stimulus for physical and psychological health, and that a social system which does not provide a life with these qualities in reasonable balance will fail them. It can be argued that our own society, with its hectic rate of change, with the breakdown of traditional social structures, with the loss of clarity in roles to be performed by its members, and its persistent pressure to the consumption of goods, has so sacrificed identity and security to the demands of stimulus that we no longer have any sense of who or what we are or any consciousness of personal or community purpose. Stimulus has become a drug to which we are so addicted that a moment of quiet or of solitude is a terror to be feared.

Our own society has not always been like this – it has become so during the last few decades only. And there are still societies in other parts of the world where men and women live in dignity and fulfilment on incomes which would seem ludicrously low to us, with little change from year to year beyond the rhythmic progression of the seasons and lacking almost all the material impedimenta of industrial society.

58

The Aboriginal people of Australia lived, and some still live, in a society of extreme material simplicity. They found both security and challenge in winning a reluctant livelihood from an inhospitable land. They found time for an artistic and ceremonial life of a richness we can but envy. In their oral traditions they built and preserved a fabric of myths expressed in story, song and ritual which expressed their intimate relationship with the land and its creatures. From Captain Cook onwards, those who have known them have wondered at their freedom from the tyranny of things and at the steadfastness of their moral and spiritual values.

There is then no fundamental reason to fear that an ecologically ordered world would necessarily fail to provide mankind with identity, security and stimulus or that it would deny stature and dignity. But it is certain that the life it would offer would be strangely different from our own and humankind would become radically different.

I have said earlier that the necessary changes and the effectiveness of the mechanisms to bring them about depend upon the establishment of a pattern of values consistent with ecological principles. I must confess, at the conclusion of this essay, to some uncertainty as to the compatibility of such values with the solutions through prices, changing economic institutions and continued economic growth which I have argued are possible. In a way I have presumed that mankind will continue to be, within this new ecological framework, still *Homo economicus*, alert, pushing, imaginative, charged with the entrepreneurial spirit, diverting libido into more ingenious combinations of known resources. But could such a creative creature at the same time accept unquestioningly the new decalogue which must begin:

- Thou shalt have no other gods before the Finite Environment!
- Thou shalt not live on capital!
- Thou shalt not lust after resources at disequilibrium prices!

This may be to presume incompatible things. A human race which has genuinely 'internalised' the convictions and the disciplines necessary to live within a finite environment might in fact prove to be worshipful, fearful, self-limiting, imaginatively timid, an acceptor of authority, and a searcher after safety. I hope not, but I cannot be sure. Whether the things I have presumed are in fact compatible is a question

59

to which the skills of economists can give no answer. Their view of human beings is too restricted.

There is much to be said for economists resuming, as some are beginning to do, the work which Malthus began so long ago. But both natural scientists and economists have a limited view of the motives which inspire human beings and of the diversity of social forms which can provide a context for the drama of their personal lives. The problems for which the ecologist demands an answer may well respond better to the analysis and the intuitions of the psychologist, the sociologist and the anthropologist. In any case we need to call in question the bases of our respective disciplines.

4

Science and Technology –
For What Purpose?

Originally presented as the keynote address to the Australian Academy of Science, Canberra, ACT, April 1979. Subsequently presented at the Centre for Resource and Environmental Studies, Australian National University, Canberra, ACT, April 1979.

T HE title 'Science and Technology – For What Purpose?' puts the question in a form which links science and technology, thus implying that they are both directed to a single and common end. It is true that politicians, bureaucrats, businessmen and even many scientists tend to justify the activities of scientists and their claim to a share of society's resources in terms of the contribution they have made and can, presumably, continue to make to technology and thereby to the outcome of industrial production in its widest sense. But this link is historically relatively new. Even the achievements of the Industrial Revolution and the technology which made them possible were the work of ingenious practical people rather than intellectually and academically equipped scientists.

The forecasts of Bacon in the seventeenth century, that the new approach to the study of nature would transform our mastery over it, showed few signs of being fulfilled until this century. Until then scientists were concerned to observe, to describe and to understand what mankind encounters when confronting nature, rather than to answer the question, 'What must I do to achieve a desired result?' Accordingly scientists' relationship with nature remained organic, indeed familial. Both nature and the human race were God's handiwork and even if humans believed themselves to occupy a special place – being made in the image of God and therefore the crowning glory of creation – it was a place which carried obligations as well as privileges. Mankind was 'in charge of' the world of nature and this superiority, like other forms of nobility, carried the obligation of *noblesse oblige*. It is only recently that scientists generally rejected this relationship and have begun to see nature and to act in relation to it as an adversary to be conquered or a quarry to be exploited.

THE NATURE OF SCIENTIFIC ENQUIRIES

So science is not a homogeneous set of activities. There is science for understanding and science for manipulation and while they merge into one another – and the former frequently now provides the basis for the latter – their styles and motivation are different. Science for understanding is an expression of human curiosity – the need to devise an intellectually graspable model of the natural world which enables us to find our way around in it, to think about it coherently and to realise how the things we observe 'hang together'. Emotionally the development of such intellectual models derives from the sense of wonder in the face of nature and has much in common with the creative work of artists. The tests by which the models are judged are concerned not only with their compatibility with observed facts and their powers of prediction but also with their simplicity and elegance – tests which are essentially aesthetic. Indeed it may well be true that none of these models, even those most highly prized and most widely accepted by scientists, are compatible with all the known observed facts. The facts which do not fit tend to be pushed aside for later consideration or until their frequency compels the design of a new model into which more of them can be accommodated.

Science, in this sense of the search for understanding, does not, in my view, need to be justified by the greater power it confers on humankind. It is its own justification as a source of enlightenment and liberation: as a noble expression of the human spirit. A society which fails to give it opportunity and scope will be thereby the poorer. And a society which demands of its practitioners that they subordinate their imagination to the priorities of the accountant, the official and the military machine will destroy their creativeness as surely as if it imprisoned them in concentration camps.

This is not to suggest that science motivated by the desire to manipulate aspects of the world in which we live has nothing in common with science for understanding or that it does not have a legitimate place among human activities. Rather it is to suggest that their purposes are different, the attitudes of mind of those who practise them may well conflict and, above all, that science for manipulation must be justified by its results. It should be required to demonstrate that the benefits it confers outweigh their costs – material, social and spiritual.

In a paper entitled 'Science, Value and Meaning' delivered at a symposium in honour of Macfarlane Burnet, Judith Wright (1975: 196), the wisest of Australian poets, saw this conflict not merely as that between scientists and literary artists. It is also the expression of the internal conflicts between the two sides of human nature; on the one hand the creative and the imaginative, which is shared by scientists, inventors and practitioners in the arts, and on the other 'the mechanic or materialistic, the manipulative, power-hungry side of us which seizes on the achievements of science and transforms them into machinery for uses which scientists, as well as artists, often cannot help but deplore'.

I find this concept of a conflict *within* human beings rather than necessarily *between* them helpful. It acknowledges the complexity of human nature and the contributions which different and indeed opposing components of it can make to the richness of human experience. Even conflict is not without its place. Between such opposites in the world and in ourselves there is a tension which sharpens our sensitivity, increases our self-awareness and stimulates our creative imagination. Ideally the tension between the desire to understand and the urge to manipulate the world to human advantage should be creative in this way. Above all the concept suggests that human beings are capable, as whole persons, of using that tension to reconcile the conflict.

If I understand Judith correctly, she is saying that the conflict has become one-sided, that tension is being lost as the materialism of successful technology overwhelms the creative imagination in a kind of 'final solution' which involves a death sentence for what is best in the human spirit. She quotes from Professor Karl Jaspers (1953):

> It is the Age of Technology, which seems to leave nothing standing of what man has acquired in the course of millennia in the way of methods of work, forms of life, modes of thought and symbols . . . we today, misunderstanding ourselves, see ourselves in our technological ability as creators of salvation on earth without parallel – or we see ourselves as equally without parallel in our spiritual perplexity.

Since those words were written the perplexities have multiplied and become more pervasive.

THE ROLE OF TECHNOLOGY IN OUR LIVES

To judge whether the anxieties induced by these perplexities outweigh the benefits of the material salvation technology has made possible, it is necessary to consider the role and influence of technology in shaping not merely the product of our economic system, the achievements it has made possible and the costs which it has imposed, but also the effect of its methods on the institutional structure of our society, and on the lifestyle and values of those who compose it. Only then, as whole persons, can we pass a judgement which involves effectively the imaginative and the materialistic sides of our nature.

By the term 'technology' in this consideration I mean the combination of know-how and tools which people use in productive activities – a combination which has in recent decades been derived increasingly from the application of scientific knowledge. It covers, therefore, a range which comprehends at one extreme the Australian Aborigines' spear and their knowledge of the habitat and behaviour of the animal they hunt and, at the other, the nuclear reactor and the knowledge necessary for its construction and for the safety procedures it demands. It is important to bear in mind that technology does not simply design tools or create hardware – it brings an idea and a tool into creative association.

The power and significance of such combinations can be best illustrated by example. At certain critical stages in human history, technological developments have occurred, perhaps stimulated by the need to deal with population pressures or to respond to major environmental changes, which made necessary a revolution in the whole lifestyle of the peoples affected. Thus the realisation that plants and animals could be domesticated, and the yield of food increased by the use of primitive tools for cultivation, brought with it the replacement of hunter-gatherers with their seasonally controlled, nomadic life, by shepherds and gardeners. We are inclined, long after the event, to think of this change as a step up in the material progress of mankind and as a source of a richer, more satisfying life. In the long run this seems to have been true, but in the early stages of the transition the opposite was more likely. The pressure of population on the food which could readily be hunted or gathered would have been urgent and immediate. The command over the new technology and its potential product would have been tentative and halting – the lessons difficult to learn and their promise uncertain and often unfulfilled. The story of the Fall of Man and his being cast out of the Garden of Eden to earn his bread by the sweat of his brow may well be a mythological version of that first technological revolution. It is a story which records our nostalgia for the golden age in which God's natural garden was adequate for all needs. Certainly Aboriginal Australians, who for tens of thousands of years had lived richly on the yield of that garden, now, despite their interest in selected aspects of non-Aboriginal technology, share that nostalgia.

The replacement of handicraft by mechanical tools in the textile and metal-working industries in the Industrial Revolution destroyed a way of life in which handicraft fitted into a largely self-sufficient peasant agriculture. The closing of the commons made the peasant landholders into a landless proletariat dependent for income on the work of the 'dark Satanic mills'. There can be little doubt that for generations the impact of that technological revolution was profoundly damaging to the health and welfare of the majority of the working-class British. Indeed it may well have remained so had not the colonisation of the new world and access to wider markets brought cheaper food and placed the British workers in a privileged position from which they could demand a greater share in the affluence of their employers.

INDUSTRIAL SOCIETY – THE TRIUMPH OF MATERIAL CONSUMPTION AS THE DETERMINANT OF THE GOOD LIFE

It was, however, this revolution which in due course achieved the most fundamental social changes from which derive most of the characteristics of contemporary industrial societies – the development of the conviction that it is by the possession and consumption of commodities purchased through the market that the quality of life can be improved. The application to production of the principle of division of labour – the breaking down of the activities into small separate uniform processes – made possible great increases in efficiency. It enabled greater skill to be developed in the performance of individual processes, more effective tools to be designed, advantage to be gained from the special qualities of the region in which production was carried out, from the special aptitudes of workers and from the ingenuity and energy of managers and entrepreneurs. All these factors contributed to economies of scale which encouraged the emergence of increasingly large enterprises, the concentration of decision-making in fewer hands, standardisation of products and the need for mass markets to demand and consume them. The result over many decades has been the appearance of a great flood of commodities of enormous diversity and ingenuity catering for human needs and fancies at prices with which the traditional crafts could not compete. The export of these commodities provided the resources to buy cheaper food and exotic luxuries from the whole world, which also appeared as commodities to be purchased in the shops and markets of industrial society.

The prosperity which technological leadership and organising and trading skills brought to Britain, combined with the growing bargaining capacity of the workers, meant that the benefits of this revolution could be shared widely in Britain and subsequently in Europe and America as these nations took over the principles of the division of labour and developed the technology which it had made possible. In these countries there is little doubt that the industrial commodity age has been – and has been felt to be for the great majority – a period of fulfilment in which new and richer experiences and opportunities were opening up

66

for those who composed that majority. Until relatively recently these benefits could reasonably be seen as net additions to human welfare, at least in the industrialised countries. The newly available commodities and employment opportunities appeared to be marginal additions to a way of life which environmentally, socially and institutionally seemed largely unchanged by them. In the short run there seemed little reason to expect that these aspects would be significantly affected. Above all, experience, in due course, had come to suggest that the benefits of this rising production of commodities would gradually be shared by the poorer sections of the community (at least in industrialised countries) to an extent sufficient to ensure for them a steadily improving quality of life.

This expectation – combined with the much-advertised confidence that science and technology could provide a limitless flow of new materials, new sources of power, new knowledge, processes and tools to keep the cornucopia of commodities overflowing – provided the apparent justification for the faith in industrial society: a vision of steadily increasing material prosperity filtering down to the poorest levels and spreading progressively into less industrially developed societies across the world.

THE SHADOW SIDE – THE IMPACT OF CONSUMER MATERIALISM

Changes which are marginal in individual instances can, if widespread and continuing, transform a society and the way of life of its members. There can be no doubt that such changes have occurred in recent decades and that the pace of change has been accelerating. Many believe those changes are predominantly deleterious. Even those whose faith in the industrial society persists are more defensive and less confident in their advocacy of it.

Complaints that the rising tide of commodity production stimulated by science-based technology threatens to exhaust scarce and irreplaceable resources, and that accumulating waste and damage to the environment are rendering it progressively less suitable as a habitat for humankind and indeed for all living creatures, are now familiar. We

67

attach weight to these complaints according to the way in which we interpret the evidence and to the degree of faith we hold in the powers of technology. I do not wish to enter into that debate now but merely to remark firstly that all industrial and most agricultural processes use up natural substances which are organised in ways useful to maintain and leave useless or harmful waste to be disposed of and, secondly, that while science-based technology may extend the life of natural resources it does so predominantly by expensive capital-intensive methods. Resources, even if they are not in danger of exhaustion, appear certain to become more costly. I will return to the economic and social implications of this later.

In the meantime I wish to draw attention to some consequences of industrial production of commodities for human beings in their personal lives, consequences that flow from the way in which that production is organised and its impact on the institutions of human society.

Firstly, human beings are decreasingly necessary in industrial and agricultural production. To the extent that they remain necessary they become increasingly appendages to the machines that perform the processes involved. Opportunities to use natural abilities, to exercise judgement and initiative or to make decisions become the privilege of the few, and even for them it is a privilege which can be exercised only within parameters determined by the logic of the productive processes. Thus, for the great majority, work, which occupies the largest part of their waking hours, is an activity in which their most human capacities languish, with which they cannot identify and which provides neither security nor stimulus.

Secondly, people are polarised from one another – as a result of the concentration of the population in cities, the separation of the work context from the home, and the disappearance of social groups of manageable size within which human relations develop easily and naturally. Traditional institutions for social interaction and for the conduct of common affairs become ineffective.

Thirdly, the structure of the corporations which organise most production is essentially hierarchic. Power is concentrated in the hands of the few, accountable in only the most general and frequently the most

68

ineffective ways and then almost exclusively for the maintenance of profitability and the continuity and growth of the enterprise. Despite the absoluteness of this power it tends to be exercised without personal responsibility but rather, vicariously and impersonally on behalf of the corporation – an entity without compassion to be moved or soul to be damned. It is no wonder that mining companies can behave towards Aboriginal Australians as if they were no more than obstacles to the organisation of production, to be dealt with by the exercise of power.

Lewis Mumford (1970, Vol. 2) in *The Myth of the Machine* points out that mining

> . . . set the pattern for later modes of mechanisation by its callous disregard for human factors, by its indifference to the pollution and destruction of the neighbouring environment, by its concentration upon the physico-chemical process for obtaining the desired metal or fuel, and above all by its topographic and mental isolation from the organic world of the farmer and the craftsman and the spiritual world of the Church, the University and the City. In its destruction of the environment and its indifference to the risks to human life, mining closely resembles warfare.

Mumford's words refer to the role of mining in the creation of industrial society, but much of the quotation would still be relevant to the policies of mining corporations, even though those who decide and speak for them would in their private lives be models of concern for humankind and its environment.

Fourthly, the growth of mammoth industrial corporations has brought into being a corresponding bureaucracy to serve, monitor, regulate and police their activities. As doubts increase about their environmental and social effects the scale and intrusiveness of this bureaucracy is likely to grow more rapidly than its effectiveness and social responsibility. It is an easy transition for regulatory authorities to become the advocates – and indeed the agents within the bureaucracy and the government – of those whom it is their function to regulate. A good illustration of the way in which public institutions are moulded to serve the purposes of productive corporations is given by the educational system, whose function of providing the young with the intellectual tools for living has become predominantly the means to indoctrinate them with values appropriate to the functions and welfare of those corporations. Thus Ivan Illich (1973), a distinguished American educationist, comments:

> ... schools ... teach people the accountant's view of the value of time, the bureaucrat's view of the value of promotion, the salesman's view of the value of increased consumption and the union leader's view of the purpose of work.

Even more are these comments true of the unofficial instruments of education – radio, television, the press and advertising.

The industrial corporation has provided the model for the institutions which conduct these and other public functions. They have been developed within, and themselves embody, the principles of a system based upon division of labour, specialisation of function and hierarchical authority structures. Each institution has its own purposes and powers appropriate to them. Those who make decisions within it are constrained to serve its purposes – the primary one being the continuity and power of the institution itself. Decisions, once made within one institution, become data for others. Despite the interrelationship of these institutions and the fact that they are designed to serve society in *all* its purposes for the benefit of the men and women composing it, decisions are rarely, if ever, made by (so to speak) a *whole* man or woman but by a man or woman acting vicariously for a specialist institution within the limits of its purposes. Furthermore, those institutions will powerfully have moulded the values and ways of thought of those who run them. I think there is evidence that these institutions tend to turn people – both those within them and those affected by them – into accessories. Power and decision-making capacity are concentrated in the hands of those who identify themselves most absolutely with the institution, its bureaucracy and the values which are congenial to its purposes.

Finally, accelerating change destroys the balance between stability, change and tradition, undermining the basis of our institutions of law and political action. The relevance of shared memories, of traditions, of

70

collective myths and of honoured precedents to decisions and choices is destroyed. Political institutions valid for the societies in which they developed become meaningless in societies which bear little relationship to them. Thus the practice and theory of democracy evolved in communities small enough for wide participation in discussion and decision-making to be a reality. There is little evidence of such participation in modern representative democracy.

It is these organisational effects of industrial society which have produced the scale and complexity of our institutions. So pervasive is their power that almost all significant decisions are made within them, constraining the scope for individual choice and initiative. It is because of their influences that the choices which we make, or which are made for us, seem invariably to come down on the side of the most materialist and power-hungry of human aspirations – that 'the good that we would we do not and the evil we would not we do'. Thus, although we know intellectually that every society needs both stability *and* change, tradition *and* innovation, justice *and* compassion, growth *and* decay, we reject the tension between them in favour of a 'final solution'.

The impact of these changes on the individual, the family and other social and traditional groupings impairs the quality of the lives open to them. It makes ineffective the choice between conceivable lifestyles and above all destroys those ways of looking at the world to which human societies have turned to find meaning and purpose in life, leaving little or nothing but the hope of an increasing flow of commodities to replace them. For many even this hope may prove ephemeral. The belief that the productivity of the industrial system would, by the inherent processes of that system, be filtered down to be shared by the lowest strata of workers was based on a few decades in the experience of Britain, the United States of America and some western European countries. Even there, the benefits enjoyed were derived in part from the exploitation of the inhabitants of less industrialised countries whose resources and labour were obtained in exchanges heavily weighted by monopoly power in the interests of those already industrialised and commercially organised. Within these countries themselves the circumstances had been unusually favourable. In the early stages of industrialisation, enterprises could be established without great capital and, with the

71

colonisation of the New World, natural resources were freely open for exploitation, while at home coal as a source of power appeared unlimited. Profits were good and, as the entrepreneur's capital accumulated, and economies of scale, together with improved technology, made possible falling unit costs of production, he was able to yield to the pressure of increasingly organised workers for a larger share of the cake. Later, confidence in the burgeoning fecundity of science and technology in ensuring continued cheap materials and rising productivity seemed to justify the expectation that this state of affairs was inherent in our industrial system and could be counted on to continue.

However, in recent years radical changes have emerged. Some basic natural resources have become scarce – if not to the point of disappearance, then to the point where their proprietors can exact from organisers of production a rent-like charge for their use. Such exactions are likely to become increasingly common and severe as resources become more scarce.

In addition, the need to pursue more remote and difficult sources of natural resources requires more complex and costly technology and, therefore, greatly increased capital. As a result capital is in short supply and commands a price which, by historical standards, is high.

When specialised know-how and control over the processes of innovation become increasingly significant in production, it also emerges that they are controlled by patent rights and so are private property, usually of corporations. Payment must be made for access to such knowledge or information, and the prices which the entrepreneur must meet will depend on the importance of the information concerned and the absoluteness of the control exercised over it by its owner.

The organisers of production, therefore, are confronted with demands, from the owners of these two major factors in their processes, for a greater share of the proceeds. This obviously affects both their capacity and willingness to provide an increasing share to those who supply the labour they employ or who supply them with materials and food which are produced from renewable resources. Indeed, if the exactions of proprietors of scarce material resources, of capital and increasingly of information, eat into their returns, so as to reduce them below traditional expectations, they will feel compelled not merely to

72

resist wage earners' demands but to try to reduce real wages. There is good reason to believe that the falling level of real wages, expressed in terms of its purchasing power over commodities during the last few years, reflects just such a response by businessmen. Opinions differ about whether this check to the rise in wage earners' real income is temporary – a halt to enable an 'overhang' of earlier 'excessive increases' to be eliminated – or whether it reflects a continuing change in the distribution of the product of the economic system.

TECHNOLOGY – THE IMPACT OF ITS OWNERSHIP AND CONTROL

Faith in the capacity of science and technology to enable the system to continue to deliver a growing volume of desired commodities is the basis of optimism about the capacity of the economic system to continue to meet our expectations of a rising level of real income for even the poorest citizens. Whether one shares this optimism depends on whether one shares the faith on which it is based. In the long run there must be a physical limit to the production of material goods and it seems most improbable that we will not at some point reach the stage of diminishing returns from the application of knowledge to the means whereby this is achieved. But in the shorter run the issue will probably be determined by the capacity of wage earners (employed and unemployed) to secure a proportionate share of whatever increase in the total product technology makes possible. This will turn on the answers to the following questions. Firstly, who owns and controls the tools, techniques and information in which technology is embodied for productive purposes, and by what processes are its benefits allocated? Secondly, is the bargaining power of wage earners sufficiently strong for them successfully to negotiate their share of those benefits?

Let us consider the second of these questions. There can be no doubt that in most industrialised countries, including Australia, the bargaining position of most wage earners has been seriously weakened in recent years, for the following reasons. Firstly, the enterprises employing them face increasing charges for access to scarce resources and rising needs for increasingly expensive capital. If the return to the entrepreneur is to be sustained, it must, unless the benefits of new technology are rising correspondingly, be recovered from the share of labour – there is no other source and the entrepreneur's bargaining stance will be correspondingly tough. Secondly, the current pattern of technological change concentrates heavily on labour-saving developments particularly from the application of computer and other information-based technology, and as a consequence there is widespread and growing structural unemployment. Thirdly, the general state of the world economy is uncertain even where temporary improvements have appeared. This can be seen as the result of an unwillingness of businesses to venture or expand until the level of return to them has been restored to that which they consider adequate. Alternatively, businesses may support policies directed to maintaining a level of unemployment sufficient to ensure acquiescence among wage earners generally to the reduction in their real wages.

Such acquiescence, even if it is achieved overall, will not be completely general. It is characteristic of labour-saving technology, particularly the most highly capitalised and sophisticated, that it becomes dependent upon the skills, or sometimes merely the presence, of a small number of operatives whose absence can immobilise the whole enterprise or even the whole community. Such operatives are, like the proprietors of scarce resources, in a monopoly position and therefore able to exact a significant share of the total product as the price of their services. However, proportionately, those in the fortunate position are a small minority.

Furthermore, the bargaining power of wage earners in the industrial countries is also being weakened by the internationalisation of the employment aspects of the production process. It is now frequently possible, especially for transnational corporations, to distribute the various phases of their production so as to take advantage of the most favourable labour conditions from their point of view, taking into account not merely special skills, aptitudes and experience, but also the general level of wages and the aggressiveness of union leadership and organisation. This possibility will tend to equalise wage levels between countries, and in current circumstances equalisation seems more likely to be achieved by a reduction or slowing down of increases in wage rates in established industrial countries, rather than by a speeding up of increases in those slowly emerging or less industrialised.

Let us consider where ownership and control of technology in fact lie and how this affects the distribution of the total product. New science-based technology can emerge from the ingenuity of individuals, from research conducted in universities and similar public institutions, or from the organised research and development programs within existing firms. It can, through the patent laws, become the property of its developers who can for a period make exclusive use of it, sell it or allow its use by licence for a royalty. Patents lapse in due course and in theory at least the technology involved becomes freely available to all users. Much potential technology, the outcome of research in public institutions such as CSIRO and universities, is freely available to all.

But ownership of, or access to, technology – free or patented – is rarely enough in itself. To make use of it effectively requires an understanding of how it fits into or can change existing technology or the pattern of production, the know-how to achieve such adaptation, and frequently access to substantial capital and an organisation which can carry through the pilot model stage, mount an expensive production program and market the resulting product. Few innovators take their new technology through all these stages. Every university and research institute knows that its best chance of deriving reasonable reward for innovations is to share them with established commercial corporations. In the bargaining process the weight of advantage leans heavily on the side of the potential user. He must commit large resources to developing and marketing the innovation, and he bears the risk of failure, so his share of the reward must be assessed accordingly. Those who produced the innovation lack the organisational resources to act independently. At best they can only choose between a limited number of potential users. Yet this process ensures that most new knowledge or technology becomes predominantly the property of existing, large, powerful corporations and that they will be able to extract a corresponding share of the extra product it makes possible. Even the provision that patents lapse, making their content freely available, does little to impair this monopoly advantage. Its corporation owner is in a strong position to ensure that by the time the patent has lapsed it is either followed by another patentable development or is protected by knowledge, the development of which by others would be slow and expensive.

In oversimplified words, technology in our society is the property of large corporations and, like the ownership of scarce resources, it confers on its possessors the capacity to exact a rent-like tribute from the final product as a price for its use. Therefore only the surplus over that tribute is available for the entrepreneur to bargain for division with the labour which he employs. In that bargaining most wage-earners have few and anything but splendid cards to play. Similarly, the poor countries cannot compete with the rich except by offering cheap and acquiescent labour.

In an equally weak position are those, many of them in less industrialised countries, who primarily with their own labour and the renewable resources of the sun and the soil produce foodstuffs and raw materials for sale to industrial corporations. They own nothing which is protected by monopoly – neither from scarcity nor from legal or economic strength. To them the power of technology must seem a perpetual threat and the need to sell their product in the open markets of the world an invitation to a game in which all the aces are in the other hands.

We have, I believe, been misled by our experience with the economic system in industrialised countries over the last 150 years. Its success has been due largely to temporary circumstances: to the running down of exhaustible resources; to ignoring the accumulating costs of pollution and other environmental damage; to the exploitation of the populations of non-industrialised societies; and, in our own communities, to the exploitation of women and other minorities.

We may perhaps cheerfully dismiss the doomsayers, like the Club of Rome, who foresee early physical exhaustion of the world's resources, but we cannot ignore the prospect that private and corporate ownership of property in land, scarce resources, technology, expertise and information of all kinds, as well as in rare skills and capacities, will lead to increasing concentrations of wealth, income and power, balanced by increasing poverty at the other end of the socio-economic scale. The extreme end of that scale may be in other societies, but our own will not be wholly immune.

In politically mature societies, it is perhaps not inevitable that polarisation of affluence and poverty should develop as absolutely as I have described. John Stuart Mill, more than a hundred years ago, recognised that as a consequence of the increasing scarcity of agricultural land in England, landowners were placed in a monopolistic position and able to exact rent as a price of access to their land. He remarked that this monopoly could not be prevented but that it was possible that the rent from it could be held in trust for the benefit of the community. The relevance of his comments was apparently dissipated as the colonisation of new lands and, later, science and technology pushed that prospect of scarcity of land into the background. That relevance has now re-emerged dramatically along with increasing scarcities of other natural resources. It is not beyond the wit of our society to channel some part of these rent-like exactions so that they can be held in trust for the community's benefit. If we fail to achieve this, technology and science will become exclusively the handmaidens of the rich and powerful.

It is strange that, just when we are coming to doubt the validity of the faith in the division of labour and the power of technology, we are urging this combination so forcefully upon the poorer, less industrialised countries of the world. If we in Australia, with 200 years of experience, find the impact of technological change more than our society can adapt to, how much more destructive must such change be in societies whose pattern of life, social processes and view of the world are tied so strongly to tradition?

Every technological development poses for the society into which it is introduced a learning process, requiring not merely new skills and patterns of behaviour, but often also radical changes of institutions and beliefs. It is a fundamental principle of pedagogy that one must move step by step from the known to the unknown. Jean-Jacques Rousseau, perhaps the most sensitive of educational theorists, expressed this idea in its most absolute form when he said that one cannot teach what is not already in the mind of the learner. No technological change can, therefore, be comprehended and absorbed into the lifestyle and institutions of a society where the roots on which it must grow do not already exist. Attempts to go faster than this will do more damage than good – certainly in the short run and perhaps for generations or even for centuries.

Should we not, therefore, in purporting to help those of the third world, acknowledge in due humility that the limit of technological change which can benefit those now living is that which can be comprehended within and is compatible with their present lifestyle without radical change in institutions or beliefs?

Of course more than this is acceptable if we apply only the measure of the gross national product, or if we see the great affluence of the elite in these countries as an adequate compensation for the continued impoverishment of the already poor. What reason have we to believe that technological change in these countries will not be marked by the polarisation of affluence and poverty which, in its early decades, it produced in our own society?

But in justice it is not for us to decide. Let us stand ready to provide the knowledge, the ideas and the tools which the people of these lands, as persons, as producers and as communities, want to enable them to do better what they now do, to preserve their independence and to modify their way of life only as they would themselves desire; making sure that the choices are in fact those of the men and women directly concerned. A country will achieve self-reliant development to the extent that it acquires and expands its own technological base, consciously choosing those fields in which the process can grow roots. The indigenous technological tradition should not be discarded.

CONCLUSIONS

However, even if the distributional failures of the industrial society were moderated, there would remain the more human problems to which I have referred earlier – the emptiness of that part of life concerned with work, the polarisation of people from one another, the concentration of authority and power in the hands of the few, the spreading bureaucracies, the destruction of traditional values and the breakdown of the balance between stability, tradition and change, all of which have combined to diminish our society's cohesion and sense of purpose.

It is necessary, I believe, to question the basic assumptions on which industrial society rests – that increasing quantities of commodities of themselves add to human welfare; that the indirect costs of the division of labour, specialisation and the domination of human affairs by the market can safely be ignored. There is good reason for that questioning. Any serious consideration of the factors which contribute to the quality of human life indicates that psychic income – the response of the whole human person to continuing experience – derives from many factors which form no part of either their money income or the commodities which can be purchased with it.

The first conclusion, therefore, about the purposes of technology is that the question posed should be 'Science and technology – for whom?' We must recognise that the final product of our economic and social system is people living in an environment and, consequently, that the role of science and technology should be to ensure to those people the best possible quality of life.

Essentially this life consists of a succession of activities performed in their related physical and social contexts. Those activities must yield not merely survival but also physical and psychic health and joy in living. The degree to which they do so will depend on the nature and quality of those contexts, on the personal relationships which are established within them and on whether the activities and contexts yield a reasonable balance between privacy and a sense of belonging, between security and challenge, between mankind's own personal achievement and its compatibility with whatever faith we may hold about the purpose and justification of life.

It is possible to identify the factors upon which quality of life depends and to assess usefully the scope for them which society offers its citizens. It is possible, therefore, to assess the impact which any technological changes will have – not merely on the quantity and quality of commodities available to the community but also on the whole lifestyle as expressed in the combinations of activities and contexts it offers its citizens. This assessment can be made only by 'whole' men and women, not by those who are the instruments or the accessories of institutions of limited purpose.

Such an assessment now leads, I believe, to an inevitable conclusion that industrial society increasingly denies many of its citizens the opportunity to choose and make effective a lifestyle which provides physical and psychic health and joy of living. This result has emerged because the consequences of the dominant concept of division of labour backed by science and technology, other than those which are reflected in the output of commodities, have been largely ignored or accepted as inevitable. Those ignored consequences have led inexorably to threats to the environment, to increasing scarcities of basic resources, to concentrations of wealth, income and power and to unmanageable giantism in the social structure.

It is not necessary that science and technology should serve such purposes. Already increasing numbers of those concerned are turning their attention to considering some of the more obvious side-effects of the concentration on commodities. There are serious efforts to reduce waste, to economise on capital, to extend the lives of durable goods, to recycle materials and so on. But these deal with symptoms rather than the disease.

In recent years technological change has given increasing emphasis to the use of information and to its role in modifying the products of the economic system and especially in reducing our demands for scarce material resources. Some see this shift of emphasis as heralding a new economic society – the 'post-industrial' or 'information society'. The new emphasis is already apparent to some degree and has some encouraging aspects. The desire and the capacity to economise on materials, and above all on energy, are indeed welcome. Properly used, information technology can, in theory at least, make management better informed, more intelligent and more humane, and could bring producers and consumers closer together. It would indeed be useful if those entrepreneurs who realise its potential in these aspects prove to be the most successful.

This trend demands careful study. There is much to be learned about it. It should be noted, however, that it does not question the current belief that 'progress' is best expressed in our increasing flow of commodities. It does not question the belief that the market is always the best guide to the use of resources. Above all it ignores the fact that information, like other forms of technology as well as material resources and capital, will continue generally to be the property of the wealthy. Increased emphasis on information will do little to counter the effects of scarcity on the distribution of income in favour of proprietors. It will not of itself ensure that its benefits are shared by, or held in trust for, the community generally. Furthermore, the impact of information technology on the work experience of those who will be involved in its processes, and the quality of life generally of those in our society who are most at risk, remains to be explored. It is still necessary, therefore, to ask whether it can qualify the dominance of the market; whether it can offset the effect on human life of the division of labour and specialisation; whether it can reduce the growing concentrations of power which, from our experience, we know will be abused.

In historical periods leading up to dramatic or revolutionary change it is possible after the event to discern precursors which foreshadow the pattern of that change. These precursors are much less easy to recognise before or even during the process of change itself. But I wonder whether it may not be significant that growing numbers of people are seeking voluntarily to form groups small enough for those within them to care for and help each other; for self-reliance of individuals and of groups to be more significant; and for producer and consumer to be more often the same person. In other words, that increasing numbers seek to escape, in part at least, from the tyranny of the division of labour and from the complexities and polarisation it ultimately leads to. It may be in the varied, voluntary groups emerging in societies around the world that the pattern of the future will be seen. It will be especially important in assessing the effect of the 'information revolution' to consider how far such groups will have access to this new or increased resource.

If I am right that it is in such smaller groups, communities and societies that a healthful future for mankind will be found, the challenge to science and technology will be to devise a combination of information, ideas and tools for it – a technology for persons rather than for corporations – a technology which ensures that our right to choose is not overborne by the machine or by the institutions which serve its purposes; which optimises not production but the whole quality of life. When scientists and technologists judge their own performance by these tests, the tension between the creative and materialist sides of human nature will be restored.

5

Economic and Ecological Issues
in Resource Management

Originally published in A.B. Costin and H.J. Frith (eds), Conservation,
Harmondsworth: Penguin (revised edition, 1974).

THE professional training of an economist and the experience of a
central banker are not necessarily adequate to deal with the problems of resource allocation in the public domain where the application
of economic principles is frequently inhibited by the desire to apply a
different set of values and tests of efficiency, different from those which
govern their allocation by market processes – perhaps especially in
relation to water resources from which I shall draw most of my
examples.

I propose, therefore, to look at the problem of water resource management as an example of the more general issues of resource allocation in a society whose economic system is a mixture of market-
motivated enterprise and morally or politically motivated interventions
by governments and their agents. In this I would hope to consider what
traditional economic analysis and techniques may be able to contribute,
what appear to be their inadequacies, and hopefully perhaps to suggest
where you may usefully look for help in the solution of the problems
which face you.

It is, I suppose, unnecessary to emphasise to you at any rate that
water is a scarce resource. A glance at a map of the world showing the
distribution of population illustrates very clearly the relationship

between people and water in the form of precipitation or perhaps of river flow, and in Australia it is already clear that water supply sets the effective limit to population growth in practically all parts of this, the driest continent. It is perhaps too infrequently emphasised that at least in the southern half of Australia no significant source of water remains which is not either fully used or substantially committed.

Scarcity is, of course, particularly to an economist, not an absolute. It is relative obviously to population, to the role of water in the pattern of the life which that population wishes to live and to the technology with which it is used. And I must remind you that it is relative also to the price at which the scarce commodity is supplied.

Our society is lavish, indeed extravagant, in its use of water – both in personal or domestic use and as a component in rural and industrial production. By contrast, a Central Australian Aborigine would, in his natural way of life, achieve reasonable sustenance and health with almost negligible quantities of water; human societies the world over range between those two extremes.

The techniques by which, in our society, water is supplied and drained off after use domestically are clearly wasteful as also is its use in industry. Added to this, industry and urban drainage frequently reduce the effective supply of usable water by the introduction of pollutants into natural sources of supply. There is clearly need and opportunity for greater care and for the development of more economical techniques of use especially in Australia, which is relatively so water-deficient.

It cannot be doubted that this extravagance could be restrained and more economical techniques stimulated if greater reliance were placed upon the price mechanism in its distribution. We tend to distribute water almost as if it were, like air, freely available. Few towns or cities make charges for their water which cover the cost of storage and reticulation; the rates charged to industry frequently amount to a disguised subsidy to the enterprise concerned; in rural irrigation projects the normal practice in Australia is to make no charge against the capital costs of storage but sometimes to attempt to cover reticulation costs.

At the level of domestic consumption the subsidised provision of water at low rates can be seen as providing, in uniform quantity to all people unrelated to income, a consumer good very important to the quality of life. But beyond the minimum level necessary for that quality of life, such low rates frequently operate (for example in the larger and more elaborately cared for gardens of the better off) as a subsidy to those who do not need it, and act unquestionably as a stimulus to waste.

In industry there seems to be even less justification for subsidising the use of water. The burden of such subsidy falls on the general tax-payer and the benefits are greatest to industries which are extravagant users of water. This leads to a distortion of the allocation of capital and labour in ways intensifying the shortages of water.

There seems, therefore, a good case for the revision of our present pricing policies in the supply of water. The objective of equality of access to the quantities necessary to an acceptable quality of life could be met by a 'two level' price scale while economy would be encouraged by a scale which was progressive in relation to the quantities used.

However, when all has been done through technology and pricing policy to ensure economy in the use of water there is likely to remain a problem of progressively intensifying scarcity. The distribution of population through the world and its obvious dependence on water supply is a special and critical illustration of the tendency, which Malthus first emphasised, of the human population to press upon the supply of the means of subsistence.

The limitations, especially in Australia, of water supply call in question two convictions which appear to be at the base of many national policies. The first of these is that improvements in the standard of living and of national development are dependent upon increased output of material goods. This emphasis on the goods produced for and distributed through the market reflects the values created for us or imposed upon us by the economic system within which we live and work. A moment's thought about the lives of men and women in our own or earlier ages who command our admiration and respect will demonstrate how little that admiration and respect or the quality of their lives in fact depends upon the quantity or complexity of the material goods they used. The values which determine the pattern of life within any society are not unchanging nor beyond the wit and imagination of man to comprehend, nor beyond his capacity to change. In the mythology of mankind water has at all times been a symbol not merely of sybaritic luxury, or of clinical purity, or of overflowing affluence, but also of the contemplative quiet and of the mind and spirit of man and the universe. A set of values which gave more weight to the latter group would not necessarily offer less fulfilment to the essential quality of life or opportunity for man. There is no reason why our way of life should not be guided more by such values.

The second conviction which I feel an intelligent assessment of our water resources will call in question is that there is virtue in population growth for its own sake. We cannot more than marginally add cubits to the stature of our water supply – but the use we make of it and the numbers of those who do so may to some extent be within our control. I think we ought at least to question the blind rush to multiply our numbers. Every increase in those numbers closes off another set of options, imposes a new inflexibility on the constraints that water places upon our capacity to adapt our environment to our needs.

The importance of questioning these widely held convictions is reinforced, I believe, by a consideration of the circumstances in which water is supplied to the environment in which we live and the effect which our activities may have on it.

The hydrological cycle is the infinitely complex set of mechanisms and relationships by which water is precipitated, gathered, stored and in due course evaporated and returned to set the cycle in motion once again. The complexities revealed in that cycle illustrate, in addition to the basic natural processes involved, the countless opportunities which exist within its divisions and sub-divisions to modify, to use and to abuse the functioning of the cycle itself. The cycle, therefore, must be seen not as something functioning in isolation but as part of a much more complex system or set of systems the full nature of which reflects also the impact of man and society upon the whole physical environment.

Let me illustrate the significance of this point by telling you of an experience which recently fell to my lot. At the invitation of the forestry authorities in Western Australia I recently visited the forests of the south-western area of that state. The purpose of the visit was to see something at first hand of the context of the proposed woodchip enterprise about the economics of which I had expressed some doubts. My doubts at that stage were essentially economic in the narrowest sense – i.e. whether the enterprise was likely to give an adequate return on the capital – private and public – which would need to be invested in it.

I found, however, that the issues were much more complex and much more widely significant than that limited economic issue. The south-west corner of Western Australia is almost the only source of substantial and reliable rainfall in a state of extreme aridity. The streams and rivers of the region, together with the limited sub-surface supplies, represent the source upon which the water supply for the cities, as well as for the rural and industrial enterprises of the whole of the southern half of the state, depend. The quality of this water supply has already been impaired by clearing for agriculture large areas peripheral to the main forests and indeed significant areas within the forest itself. As a result, almost every stream which rises outside the forest area but flows through it has for a number of years been saline to a degree which makes it unsuitable for human use without dilution with water from less affected sources. In such a situation the possible effect of woodchip enterprise on the salinity of the streams was obviously critical.

But the proposed woodchip venture was not the only human activity bearing upon the hydrological cycle in that part of the country. Many of the tree species in the forest area were and are subject to an exceedingly destructive disease threatening the survival of much of the forest – the notorious 'die-back'. The spores which spread the fungus from which this disease derives are spread through the forest by physical action. Every visitor, every vehicle, every other piece of mobile equipment is in fact a potential instrument of destruction. Rigidly controlled hygiene can, it is believed, protect the forest in relatively well-drained areas, but rigidly controlled hygiene may well be incompatible with even the present use and exploitation of the forests.

This forest area is also the location of extensive dispersed bauxite mining. The movement of transport involved in mining intensifies the risks of die-back. The mining itself endangers the forest directly.

Although companies are committed to restoring and replanting mined areas, there is amongst those most knowledgeable profound uncertainty about the effectiveness of their programs of replanting.

This combination of developments clearly places at greater risk the quality and quantity of water which is precipitated and stored in that forest area. When account is taken also of the possible pollution effect of extensive urban development close to Perth in one of the few remaining significant sources of accessible subterranean water, there appears to be good reason for concern about the compatibility of increasing human economic activity and population with adequate and high-quality water supplies for that part of Australia.

I am not and do not pretend to be competent to judge whether the threat involved in those activities is sufficiently serious to invalidate the decisions which the companies and governments concerned have made in these matters. I mention the basis of that threat to illustrate what appears to me to be a profoundly disturbing deficiency in our capacity to make rational judgements on resource use matters of such complexity and importance.

In this instance we had a project seen initially as one concerned almost exclusively with the economic use of timber resources which proved on examination to raise potentially serious problems for those concerned with present and future water resources. It is interesting to consider the procedure by which the project was examined and the considerations upon which decisions were based.

Firstly, no serious economic cost-benefit analysis was undertaken. There was, it is true, a list compiled of subjectively assessed economic and social benefits to the region which it was hoped would flow from this enterprise. No attempt was made to set these against the costs which would have to be borne in part by the general taxpayer and in part by those who could have used the resources for other purposes. Since the company concerned has been reported as unwilling to proceed with the development unless a major part of the costs of the infrastructure – the ports, the roads, the railways, etc. – were to be borne by the State (i.e. by other taxpayers) there is a presumption that a cost-benefit analysis, even if restricted to purely financial considerations, would have been unfavourable.

There was, in addition, an environmental impact assessment carried out (I believe with reasonable objectivity) by the Department of Forests, the main protagonists for the project. This assessment sought to consider the non-monetary costs incurred as a result of potential damage to other social purposes served by the forests concerned – including the impact on water quantity and quality. This assessment was not exposed to public examination but was then examined by the Environmental Protection Authority, which, after drawing attention to the possible effects of the proposal on the catchment hydrology, stated:

> Therefore the concern of the Environmental Protection Authority persists as to whether the woodchip project may gravely jeopardise what is after all a natural resource far more vital to the people – i.e. water rather than woodchips.

However, the Authority went on to conclude:

> The Environmental Protection Authority remains unconvinced that sufficient is known about the environmental implications of the woodchip proposal for it to be completely endorsed at this point in time. Equally well … the Environmental Protection Authority is scarcely in a position to render at this stage a blanket disapproval of the project.

In the absence of such a blanket disapproval the project was authorised to proceed.

My reason for elaborating this particular case in such detail is to draw attention to several highly unsatisfactory aspects of the decision-making processes involved which are not peculiar to this project but indeed characteristic of many, if not the great majority, of resource management decisions in the public sector in Australia. These unsatisfactory aspects include the following:

- The natural resources of a region (including its hydrology) form a complex and closely interrelated pattern; an analysis which fails to take effectively into account that interrelationship in all its complexity is likely to be defective.

89

- The comments of the Environmental Protection Authority which I have quoted reveal an element in the decision which can be described as 'an inverted lottery' – a point to which I shall return and elaborate in a moment.
- The decision to proceed was reached without even a narrowly economic cost-benefit analysis. A satisfactory result from such an analysis should be a necessary, but may not be a sufficient, justification for a project.
- The decision and the means of reaching it reveal the serious lack of any systematic calculus by which full 'opportunity costs' (i.e. the benefits which are forgone by carrying out any particular project) can be assessed. Such opportunity costs include not merely the possible use of the resources in alternative forms of production but also the amenities lost or the disutilities created – including in this instance particularly the effects on the hydrology of the region.

I will not elaborate on the lack of a cost-benefit analysis since it would now be generally agreed that it is unwise to commit capital and labour on a considerable scale without such an assessment and until the means for such analyses, at least of financial costs and benefits, are readily available.

However, let me elaborate on the term I used – the 'inverted lottery' aspect of the decision. In a normal lottery the investor stands to lose the price of the ticket. This is usually small in relation to his resources and it is certain in its magnitude. Certain and small! On the other hand, he stands to gain a very large prize the winning of which, of course, he has a very small chance, i.e. the benefit is large but improbable. This is perhaps not an unreasonable exchange.

In the decision-making process I have just described the position is reversed. What can be gained is small and reasonably certain: but the price of the ticket is not known in advance and could be so high as to be ruinous. Few investors I think would be attracted by such a lottery.

It cannot, I think, be denied that a sober assessment would attach a positive value, however small, to the probability of serious hydrological damage from adding the risks of the woodchip project to the other hazards of forest die-back and mining. In other words, the cost to the

90

community of participating in this gamble is uncertain but could be very large indeed. On the other hand, what is gained? The gain is the benefit, if it exists, of using the capital and labour concerned in this project instead of in some other project. Such a gain (if it in fact eventuated) is at best marginal and it can only be substantial if there is a lack of alternatives. No one could imagine that in Australia at the present time, where there is every evidence of a widespread demand for capital, widespread shortages of labour and high rates of interest, that we lack alternatives for the use of resources.

I make these points to emphasise:

- that the lack of knowledge of the magnitude and precise probability of opportunities forgone, amenities destroyed or disutilities created is not a justification for ignoring them;
- that the practice of deciding that a project can proceed because damage *has not been proven* involves implicit but unstated assumptions about the probabilities involved;
- that only if we seek a method of assessment capable of bringing into account *all* the opportunity costs involved, the weights which should be attached to them, and the range of their probabilities, can we hope to reach rational decisions or indeed be aware of the nature and implications of the decisions we are in fact making.

The distinction between the most probable value to be attached to any particular opportunity cost and the range within which such a value may in fact fall is critical. Damage to the ozone layers of the upper atmosphere, for instance, by the operations of supersonic aircraft may in the light of present knowledge appear unlikely, but a positive even if small value would almost certainly be attached to its probability by almost any competent scientist. If, in the event of damage occurring, it would be seriously deleterious to human welfare, there is something akin to Russian roulette in allowing the risk to be incurred. It is true the revolver may have a very large number of chambers, but there *is* a bullet in it somewhere.

Last year [1973], when carrying out a review of public expenditure for the government, I criticised some decisions which had been made to support water storage projects submitted by the states. That criticism was based on the lack of assessment of the cost-benefit relationships

91

involved – and in some cases on the fact that the project had been financed and proceeded with when a cost-benefit analysis had been undertaken and had judged the project not worth the costs involved. Such analyses seem to be a minimum requirement of favourable decision, at least where public resources are involved. Cost-benefit analyses, however, do not pretend to take into account the full range of opportunity costs – particularly they ignore those which involve environmental considerations because these are difficult to measure and even more difficult to put prices on. But that does not mean that they are not real.

They tend also to ignore the degree to which resource use projects serve simultaneously several purposes. We have seen in the instance that I have quoted that a forest is not simply a source of timber. It is also a habitat for native flora and fauna; it is a source of direct human enjoyment; and it is an integral part of the natural context of the hydrological cycle upon which the quantity and quality of water supplies depend. Much the same can be said of hydrological projects. A water storage can threaten or destroy valuable scientific, wild life or aesthetic values as some argue it does in the case of Lake Pedder; it can in other instances, as I believe it does in the Snowy Mountains Scheme, bring under notice and make possible control of serious environmental threats and at the same time add to and bring within the range of many, to whom they would otherwise be closed, direct enjoyment of an incredibly beautiful part of Australia.

Similarly, cost-benefit analyses usually assess the opportunity costs involved only by the assumption that capital and labour, if not employed in the project to which the test is being applied, could be used elsewhere to give a return equal to the average of the economy generally. They leave out of account, therefore, opportunity costs which are not capable of assessment in financial terms. They cannot, for instance, take account of the destruction of a wild life habitat or the direct enjoyment of aesthetic pleasures lost except where these are capable of being identified with and measured by revenue derived from tourist traffic.

An additional complication arises where the cost-benefit analyses are based on the use of estimated discounted cash flows (as most in Australia are). In this technique the purpose is to express all future receipts and payments in terms of their present financial equivalent. Thus estimated future income is discounted by applying an appropriate rate of interest to the anticipated future payment. This procedure is justified by the fact that any given sum of money receivable in, say, ten years could be matched by a smaller sum now if it were invested at the prevailing rate of interest for the ten years concerned. But this discount expresses also in financial terms the human tendency to regard as less certain and to attach less significance to events which are expected to occur in the future, and the greater the time which must elapse before that event emerges, the less significance is attached to it.

The application of the technique to the opportunity costs arising out of environmental effects presents some philosophic problems. The conviction that man has some obligation to hand on to succeeding generations an unreduced inheritance in relation to the environment is basically a conviction that in certain issues in the public domain man is not entitled to make the kind of discounts upon which most cost-benefit analyses are in fact based. It is certainly true that man in his personal decisions does not always make such discounts. Man is capable, particularly in relation to institutions, of behaving in a way which shows that he attaches as much importance to the future as to the present. A moment's thought will, I am sure, bring many examples to your minds. A man deals with the problems of his children in a way which may give as much weight to their future, although he may play no part in it, as it does to other claims upon his income. The same is true about the way some men and women think about their school or university. Similarly, a good farmer will conduct his enterprise in a way which guarantees that the basic resources of the farm will be maintained beyond the time when he will remain to use and enjoy them. So it could well be that the environment makes a similar claim on man's willingness to hold future values as importantly as present values. Until he does so and until this valuation is recognised it will remain very difficult to adapt the discounted cash flow techniques of cost-benefit analysis to decision-making techniques in issues where environmental factors are involved.

Apart from such philosophical problems, a calculus to provide a basis for rational decision-making in matters such as water resource management must be capable of taking into account a number of considerations:

- that water resources form part of the complex of natural resources generally and that together they constitute a system with exceedingly complex interrelationships;
- that information about the system and its workings will be uncertain and imprecise and frequently can only be expressed as falling within a range of possibilities with varying degrees of probability;
- that the outcome of possible decisions in relation to various desired ends will be a mixture of benefits gained and benefits forgone – that is of positively or negatively valued results;
- that both the assessed probabilities and the estimated results of the range of alternatives will, for the purposes of decision-making, in most cases be no better than subjective judgements on the outcome of exceedingly complex situations;
- the technique of decision-making and decision-makers must take into account that in these matters a decision cannot be avoided – that a decision to do nothing – to leave the *status quo* unchanged – is just as positive a choice as to decide upon any other single possible course of action. The *status quo* itself involves a process of change.

In some ways the decisions in resource management resemble those that have to be made in industry. If you think for a moment about the decisions that have to be made in such high-risk activities, for instance, as cattle raising in areas of extremely variable climate at times of highly and rapidly fluctuating prices you will recognise a similar situation: i.e. one involving a complex set of relationships to be taken into account of which you can know nothing for certain and about which you can form only moderately reliable judgements of probabilities. However, such problems are not wholly beyond the scope of rational analysis. Decision theory offers, among others, the technique of establishing theoretical models of situations in which multiple objectives must be met and where information can be expressed only in terms of probabilities. The objective of such a model is to suggest a solution which will maximise a selected set of values. I believe the exploration of such theoretical models for resource management, particularly those involving environmental factors, offers encouraging prospects, and will perhaps provide better guides to action than a simple cost-benefit analysis which, at the present time, at least provides the basis for most such decisions in the public area.

It is true that difficulties will arise in quantifying the components and the relationships expressed in such models because the probabilities to be attached to the various factors involved, and to the relationships between them, will rarely be agreed even between people who are knowledgeable in relation to them. In most cases the quantities to be attached to them can only be subjectively assessed. However, the method has the virtue of setting out clearly the basis on which the judgement has been made and the values which have been attached to the subjectively assessed components. It makes possible, therefore, a program of narrowing the range of differences which arise from the subjectivity of some of the judgements involved. In many of the major problems of resource management with which our society will be faced in practice, it will be usually the *general direction* of the action required which is of the greatest importance rather than its precise direction or magnitude. Once this direction has been determined and agreed, it will be possible to move towards progressively more effective decisions by a series of approximations or perhaps simply by trial and error. Once the main direction has been determined the terrors of error are very much reduced and the virtues of experiment increased.

In conclusion, I would like to try to bring together the essence of what I have been attempting to say:

- Water resources are part of a complex of natural resources the wise use of which requires that they be considered as an inter-related system.
- This system is best dealt with from a practical point of view in a regional context where the choice of the area to be regarded as a region is based upon natural ecological considerations rather than upon political or social factors.

- The resources must serve man's needs for multiple and inter-related purposes, including many of great importance but which cannot be satisfied through the market. The allocation of resources to these purposes presents especially difficult problems.
- Water managers should work closely with those who have responsibility for other and related resources – preferably organised in regional groups.
- Decisions should not be based simply upon an assessment of the most probable values of particular costs and benefits but should take account of the whole range of possible outcomes, taking into account, of course, the varying probabilities that can be attached to them.
- Particular caution should, in decision-making, be exercised when there exists a possible outcome which, even if of low probability, could involve catastrophic consequences.
- There is need for a more rational basis for decision-making in resource management than those at present employed.
- Finally, the building of theoretical models designed to throw up solutions which maximise a number of desired but competing ends may be of value in developing such a basis.

6

Resource Management and
Environmental Law

*Paper presented to the Environmental Law Association Symposium, University
of Tasmania, Hobart, Tasmania, 1985.*

W HAT are the prospects of our society, within the framework of
our economic, political and legal institutions, achieving the tar-
get of sustainability which underlies the world and national conservation strategies?

In order to answer this question we must consider how successful our
society has been in the past in achieving sustainability – especially in
relation to the use of land and other natural resources. If, as I believe,
our performance in this respect is one of tragic failure, what are the
components in the attitudes and institutions of our society from which
that failure derives? But, more importantly, are these reforms capable
of achievement, which could bring that history of failure to an end and
set our feet firmly on the path towards a sustainable society?

ABORIGINAL RESOURCE MANAGEMENT

When the first Europeans came to this continent they found, widespread, a characteristic landscape of grasslands among groves of trees –
like that, observed Mrs Macarthur, of an English nobleman's park. This
landscape provided a habitat for animals and plants of great diversity
giving a rich repertoire of food and materials for the indigenous inhabitants. Although we have only now begun to realise it, this landscape was

not 'natural'. It was, rather, the artefact of Aboriginal land management over tens of thousands of years. The primary instrument of that management was fire – the controlled burning of the bushland on a systematic, chequerboard pattern, over a cycle of years. This system, now sometimes referred to as 'fire-stick farming', protected the native plant and animal life from destruction by the periodic holocausts which would otherwise, as we have learned to our cost, inevitably occur. It also provided a habitat for human life, generally healthy, materially adequate, with ample leisure, and graced by a creative, social and spiritual culture of great richness and complexity.

Attention must be drawn to certain aspects of this pattern of Aboriginal land use. Firstly, it was adaptable to the varied physical and climatic character of the Australian continent. With appropriate variations it has been applied throughout that continent every part of which, to use Professor W.E.H. Stanner's phrase, Aborigines had humanised. It survived not merely the erratic cycles of drought and flood characteristic of much of the continent but also those longer-term changes which altered the very shape and character of the land: its coastline, its inland waterways and the pattern of seasonal and diurnal fluctuations of temperature and rainfall.

Secondly, it provided the basis for a lifestyle which was sustainable. Aborigines' demands upon the land's resources were modest, adjusted to their seasonal availability, varied to protect them against overuse by human mobility within the tribal lands, and by ritual constraints on the timing and pattern of their use.

Thirdly, it was effectively sustainable because it was based upon the individual and group acceptance of responsibility – the responsibility to know, to care for and to protect the land with which the Aboriginal group identified. These responsibilities were essential components of Aboriginal traditional law which expressed, justified and enforced them by social and spiritual sanctions.

In other words, Aborigines' relationship with the environment and its resources was designed to ensure survival: using sustainability as the key to this survival. It was sustainable from generation to generation because individually and collectively they had come to accept a responsibility for the conservation of its resources and, therefore, to

98

constrain and pattern demands made upon them, and to accept the disciplines which that responsibility implied. This acceptance no doubt reflected an awareness that their survival was dependent upon it.

NON-ABORIGINAL RESOURCE MANAGEMENT

By contrast, within only 200 years of the first European occupation, our society has already wrought great damage to the Australian environment. That occupation has seriously reduced its productive capacity and demonstrated beyond reasonable doubt that our present pattern of land and resource use is not sustainable in perpetuity and indeed is in some respects already under serious threat. Neither our community as a whole, nor those to whom we have entrusted the management of our resources, accept responsibility for their care and conservation; nor do they show a willingness to accept the disciplines that that responsibility requires. Environmental policy and law appear to be more effective in reinforcing the power of the exploiters of resources than in enforcing such disciplines upon them.

Let me illustrate. According to an assessment by Lance Woods in 1983, 51 per cent of rural land in Australia needs urgent treatment for land degradation, 22 per cent can be treated by better management practices and the remaining 29 per cent needs rehabilitation treatment as well as better management. Whether this includes those areas of land in Western Australia, Queensland and Central Australia that have been degraded to the extent of being no longer useful for production is not clear. The devastation of the western lands of New South Wales and Victoria provides well-known evidence of these effects and yet even now the clearing of more land is proceeding in even more fragile country.

The cattle industry of the tropical north and of the central arid zone shows extensive evidence of land degradation. This is perhaps best illustrated by the fact that practically the whole catchment of the Ord River in the Kimberley region of Western Australia has been withdrawn from production, declared a regeneration area and is being subjected at public cost to a program aimed at eliminating feral animals and to restoring vegetation. Many other areas in both the north and centre call for similar action. A significant proportion of the forest lands of Australia have been cleared with serious environmental damage, including salination of streams and widespread soil erosion. Forest policies are inadequate for the regeneration of such lands and/or to make provision for future forest product needs.

In the meantime, Australians seem mesmerised by the prospects of mineral exploitation. This is despite the obviously finite capacity of these resources, and despite the appalling history of the mining industry in its damage to the environment: in its contempt for the welfare and values of the people of the regions where it has worked; in the social costs it imposes on the community; and in the hazards of uncertainty to which its activities expose the community's future. A few examples from the past illustrate that history.

In the mid 1940s extravagant expectations about the peaceful use of atomic energy led to the establishment and development of uranium mining at Rum Jungle in the Northern Territory. The profits from the exercise were modest but the environmental damage was enormous. The processes used left Rum Jungle a wasteland and the Finniss River biologically dead for seventy-five kilometres, and in some ways environmentally injured throughout its length. The net final effect of the whole exercise was that the Commonwealth and Northern Territory governments have been left to design and carry out a rehabilitation program to reduce heavy metal pollution in the region at a cost to the taxpayer initially estimated at $16.2 million and as yet incomplete.

A similar cautionary tale of mining pollution is recorded in the history of Captains Flat close to the Australian Capital Territory, where finally the New South Wales and Commonwealth governments were obliged to agree to bear and share the cost of measures to abate heavy metal pollution in the Molonglo River – a problem which had been left by the miner concerned for the community to cope with.

You may think that such situations cannot now arise because of improved environmental law and its enforcement. Current disputes in the Northern Territory involving environmental issues in both the bauxite and uranium industries would show this belief to be mistaken. Information relevant to judgement about these issues is difficult and sometimes impossible to come by; much is kept closely under wraps.

But it is clear to the long-term residents of both the regions affected that the environment upon which they and their children will continue to depend is endangered. It seems clear that, to the commercial interests concerned, environmental protection in this instance is judged to be a luxury which cannot be afforded, whatever its effect on the local communities or whatever were the terms and conditions originally imposed and accepted.

It is impossible to assess accurately, in advance, the seriousness of environmental risks created by large mining projects, especially where dangerous substances are involved, notably uranium and other heavy metals. It is equally clear, however, that in many instances there is a real and finite risk of damage of disastrous proportions, even if that finite risk in percentage terms is numerically small. Miners often seem content to rely upon the fact that the risk is small and ignore the fact that a disaster is clearly within the range of probability. A numerically small probability must surely be given greater weight according to the seriousness of its effects if it in fact occurred. A bookmaker may cheerfully bet against a long chance if his possible loss is modest compared with his total resources, but if he stands to lose a fortune or his life if the long chance comes home, it would be a different matter.

No instance demonstrates the uncertainty and the gravity of risks more powerfully than the Roxby Downs project for the mining of uranium and other heavy metals. This project would use water on a vast scale. It is soberly argued by competent environmentalists and water management experts that because the area to be mined is linked with geologically unstable structures – the great Artesian Basin system and the surface waters of the Murray-Darling region – it could threaten the major water supply systems of Australia with serious depletion and perilous contamination. The reaction of those responsible for the project to this assessment has apparently been simply to say that their responsibility for environmental damage is confined to what occurs within the lease area.

Great emphasis is placed by the mining industry on its importance to the national economy – on its contribution to the gross national product, to the international income earned by its exports, and to the employment it provides directly and indirectly. There is good reason to question whether that emphasis is justified. There is urgent need for an objective study of these contributions and to whom the benefits accrue and on whom the costs fall. At the very least we should be aware that mining – even at its environmental best – is using up the nation's capital in the form of predominantly non-renewable resources. There is something wrong with an accounting system which records the running down of capital as a contribution to income. It may be justified in an emergency to sell off a piece of the farm to survive till the drought breaks, but no responsible farmer, or economist, would see it as a policy for general application.

The instances I have quoted of the effects of European management on the natural resources of this continent demonstrate that they have involved both the depletion and frequently the destruction of the productive capacity of the resources concerned. Criticism of the attitude of the relevant industries to the Australian environment is directed not only, or indeed primarily, at the effect on the aesthetic quality of that environment. It is also concerned with those industries' economic and technological competence and the effect of their attitude on the future of Australian society.

These cursory references to Australian experience of resource exploitation suggest that there can be little doubt that our record of environmental management is indeed one of tragic failure and that there is a desperate need for a national strategy which will halt and, hopefully, reverse the increasing degradation which our society has wrought on the environment.

A STRATEGY FOR NATIONAL RESOURCE MANAGEMENT

It is one thing to recognise the need for such a dramatic change of direction, and it may be easy to see the purposes which the new strategy should pursue. It is, however, quite another to identify the public and private action which will be necessary to give effect to that strategy; to produce a climate of opinion in which individuals and corporate enterprises will accept the need for it and accept the disciplines it will require.

Aboriginal communities in their traditional form were small, their members were in direct contact with their traditional land, were daily reminded of their dependence on it both by the actions required in their hunting and foraging and by the ritual which lent it spiritual significance. Where changes in their practices became necessary there were often precedents within personal or tribal memory which pointed the way, but, even where this was not so, consensus about action to be taken was possible in the small group who shared experience and understanding of the land and its needs.

By contrast in Euro-Australian society such consensus is difficult to achieve. Those whose decisions and actions bear upon the environment and its resources are to be found widely beyond the area immediately affected. Indeed, in a sense, they are spread worldwide and frequently know little or nothing of the nature or causes of the problem. Also the areas or resources threatened are never homogeneous. The costs and benefits of action to protect them, or of failure to do so, will be distributed unevenly.

Frequently decision-makers will be executives of corporations whose articles of association do not include environmental protection among their purposes. Such corporations generally regard environmental protection as a luxury to be enjoyed only in times of great prosperity, or to be referred to in their public relations material and even then to be secondary to profits.

Most importantly there still persists, especially among Australians, belief in the myth of inexhaustible resources – in the vast open spaces rich in potential and in the miracles which science and technology can perform to replace whatever becomes scarce or is exhausted. These miracles, however, daily become more difficult and more expensive.

Certainly until the community generally and the decision-makers of industry and commerce, as well as governments and their agencies, accept the facts of increasing scarcity, there is little prospect of reaching a consensus about environmental and resource policy. And unless we are able to recognise that fundamental changes are occurring in the working of the economic system we may continue indefinitely to defer necessary action 'until the restraints on the economy' are eased – to a time which will always be just beyond reach.

There seems to be an implication that such economic restraints can reasonably be seen as temporary: that they reflect merely the cyclical fluctuations to which the economic system is subject. There is good reason to question that naive view. The scarcities of fuel and other resources which have stimulated rising prices and established persistent inflation as a feature of our economy are not temporary. They are the product of the real limits to those resources. We are not, as the 1972 Club of Rome report feared, within imminent danger of these resources being exhausted, but it is impossible not to accept that owners of these resources are in a position to demand higher prices and a greater share of the gross national product. Those higher prices will sometimes stimulate new finds and technological improvements in use effectiveness, but such new discoveries will come increasingly from more remote, less rich and more capital-intensive ventures. Their demands for capital will compete with those of other industries and drive up interest rates and other costs.

In other words we are in the early stages of an era of economic change dominated by increasing scarcities of natural resources. This era will be characterised by inflationary price movements, high interest rates and radical changes in the distribution of wealth and income – generally to the detriment of those whose need is greatest and of those industries whose products are basic to human welfare.

Note should be taken of the increasing problems of farmers. Rising costs of fuel, fertiliser, transport, accounting and other fees, along with high interest rates, are pressing upon the proceeds their product earns on the competitive world market. Despite rising populations and food shortages, these proceeds do not rise correspondingly with the farmers' costs – those who need the food are too poor to buy it. This situation illustrates the social and economic difficulties which scarcities of basic resources will continue to create. There will be increasing affluence among proprietors of these resources but entrepreneurs in other industries will face mounting difficulties and there will be downward pressure on wage rates and other low incomes. These effects are the inevitable results of relying solely on market prices to ration scarce resources.

104

To the extent that these pessimistic expectations are realised, the need for the careful management of our resources will become even more urgent. But the way to that end is not easy. Australians generally lack a commitment to conservation. The factors I have referred to earlier make industry resistance to environmental control more effective. Even where regulatory authorities are established, as they have been in some mining legislation and agreements, they have tended to accept the industry view that regulatory action should not seriously interfere with production or profits. An American expert on the machinery of government once remarked, 'The trouble with regulatory authorities is that by the time they understand the problem they have become part of it'.

Experience with environmental impact statements (EIS) suggests that their use is frequently cosmetic and rarely influences the conduct of those responsible for the enterprise concerned. In any case, most land use is not normally subject to EIS requirements, and indeed the prevailing view seems to be that outside urban areas, landholders should be free to use their land completely at their own discretion.

If environmental control is to become more effective much more powerful measures will be necessary and these must be backed by a public opinion educated in the need for them and the urgency of achieving sustainable resource use. The essence of such policies must be that resource industries and land-users generally should be fully and continuously accountable for their activities. All enterprises involved in resource industries should be required to prepare and submit resource and environmental management plans and to revise these progressively in the light of experience. Approval of these plans by an appropriate, independent authority should be a condition for the conduct of the enterprise, and the authority should have the power to halt production pending the revision of plans which have, in its view, proved inadequate.

Similarly, land-users including farmers and pastoralists should be required to prepare land-use management plans and submit them to a conservation authority for its approval, with loss of taxation privileges and other penalties being imposed as sanctions against failure to submit and adhere to acceptable plans. Where mining is involved, management plans should also cover measures for control of use and the development of alternative technologies.

Such measures will be seen by many as gross interference in the rights of property owners and as an abandonment of the contemporary policies of 'deregulation' – especially as they would need to be supplemented by other measures to redistribute income. In truth, they would run counter to prevailing political and economic ideologies of deregulation. However, if the economic system is to continue to provide a basis for human livelihood at socially acceptable standards, it is critical that proprietors of resources accept that they hold those resources as custodians 'in trust' for the community as a whole. Their proprietorship is not an intrinsic natural right. It is, as John Stuart Mill wrote more than a century ago, part of the 'arrangements of society' – arrangements which are not immutable. Unhappily, to achieve changes in our society which would create such a custodial relationship towards the environment would require an intellectual and moral revolution. It is hard not to be pessimistic.

7

The Quality of Life and Its Assessment

Paper given at the Sixth Conference of Economists, University of Tasmania, Hobart, May 1977. University of Tasmania Occasional Paper 11.

E CONOMISTS and others have come increasingly to doubt the assumption implicit in so much of their analysis and advice that increased production is a direct and approximately proportionate addition to human well-being. Their doubts arise partly from awareness of costs, particularly of an environmental kind, which are ignored in market processes. They arise more fundamentally from an awareness that the market provides only part of the components of any lifestyle. Increasing attention, therefore, has been directed in recent years to the concept of the quality of life and to the search for ways of assessing it.

My own doubts have been influenced by my experience, direct and vicarious, with contemporary Australian Aboriginal communities. Traditionally these communities engaged in little production but depended on harvesting the natural products of the land and its waters. They neither tilled nor seeded the earth; they domesticated only the dingo and their tools were few.

It has been common to assume that their way of life was poor and degraded – 'nasty, brutish and short'. Yet social scientists have shown that while it was dependent on strict control of numbers and the average lifespan was short, those who survived infancy were usually healthy, vigorous and self-reliant. Furthermore, they have shown that this lifestyle was compatible with diverse physical and intellectual activity and a rich cultural experience. In other words their judgement frequently would have been that, while the Aboriginal lifestyle was markedly different from our own, it was capable of satisfying the physical and psychic needs of those who lived it and of providing a rewarding sense of well-being.

Thus Richard Gould (1969: 90), an American anthropologist who lived with and studied an Australian Aboriginal hunter-gatherer group, wrote:

> ... in the context of the desert environment, the daily lives of the nomadic Aborigines are essentially harmonious and rewarding. An individual grows up realising what is expected of him. By acquiring and developing practical knowledge and skill he learns to fulfil these expectations and is rewarded immediately by his own satisfaction in achievement and in the long run esteem of his kin.

Furthermore, their contact with our own more materially affluent society has generally been adverse. On cattle properties, on missions and on government settlements, culture contact usually meant for Aborigines an easier and increased access to certain food and other goods. Yet it was in almost all cases destructive. Easier and more plentiful supplies of food and other material goods were not in themselves sufficient to improve the quality of Aboriginal life.

There is now a significant body of writing about the quality of life and the search for measurable indicators of it. In that literature the more perceptive analysts, it seemed to me, were conscious that their work was handicapped by the lack of a hypothesis about factors which determined that quality and their interrelationship. Until such a conceptual framework had been developed the search for measures of assessment was likely to be fruitless.

HUMAN LIFESTYLE AND ENVIRONMENT

Obviously the factors contributing to the quality of life are many and complex, and the particular mixes desired, needed or enjoyed by different individuals will differ widely. Diversity and the opportunity to choose will obviously be important if individual preferences are to be met. Nevertheless, it seems reasonable to assume that humankind has many needs, physical and psychic, in common although they can be satisfied differently. Speculation, therefore, about the nature of those needs and the capacity of different lifestyles to meet them may lead to the formulation of relevant hypotheses. This essay can be seen as a tentative groping for such hypotheses.

It is obvious that human experience has many components – physical, biological, social, economic, cultural and, for some at least, spiritual. All of these components refer to the interaction between individuals and their environment. As Rene Dubos (1965: xviii, xix) notes:

> Human life is thus the outcome of the interplay between three separate classes of determinates: the lasting and universal characteristics of man's nature which are inscribed in his flesh and bone: the ephemeral conditions which man encounters at any given moment; and last but not least man's ability to choose between alternatives and to decide upon a course of action.

Used in this way the term 'environment' is very comprehensive. It refers not merely to the natural physical context within which the individual lives but also to:

- the accumulated physical results of mankind's past activities;
- the other living organisms which constitute the ecosystem of which people also form a part;
- the other human beings organised in groups and institutions to which the individual also belongs;
- the culture of a society; its language, the vast accumulation of knowledge, custom and beliefs, the traditional stories, songs and dances as well as the works of creative artists; and
- the economic system together with its accumulated products.

While its relevance is perhaps not so obvious to us, the pattern of beliefs means for many communities that the supernatural world is as pervasive and significant a part of their environment as the physical, social and cultural components. 'Man needs the unfathomable and the

109

infinite just as much as he does the small planet, which he inhabits' (Dostoevsky quoted in Dobzhansky, 1962: 319). This view of the environment may be important in considering the role of the economic system. The output of that system forms part of the environment, which includes not merely human-made modifications of the natural environment – cultivated fields, domesticated animals, buildings, roads and bridges, villages and cities, transport and communications systems, and so on – but also the consumable goods on the shelves of the village store, the supermarket and the domestic cupboard or pantry.

This vast array which constitutes the total environment can be seen as potentially providing a flow of services yielding satisfactions which contribute to the nature and quality of human experience. The relationship necessary to obtain these services will vary, as will also its effects on the environment. The relationship requires some form of behaviour. In its simplest form such behaviour derives from the instinctual genetic inheritance. Thus a baby responds to the stimulus of contact with the air with the reflex act of breathing. Other forms of behaviour are learned to some degree, although it seems probable that some will prove easier to learn than others: those which, during our evolutionary development, have been important to the survival of the species. Work by Jean Piaget and others on child development, and by Lenneberg and others on the development of language, supports the view that the human organisms possess structures which at the appropriate stage of maturation function to facilitate the learning of such behaviour.

The present pattern of human life has emerged only in the last few hundred years and much of it within the last few decades – too few generations to have significantly affected our genetic makeup. Even if account is taken of agricultural or nomadic pastoralist phases, these were also of relatively short duration, covering perhaps 10,000 years compared with at least 500,000 during which *Homo sapiens* has existed as hunter-gatherer and with perhaps several million years during which human-like primates have lived in a very similar style. It seems probable, therefore, that it was only because of the hunter-gatherer lifestyle that mankind had time to adapt genetically and consequently can most readily learn the appropriate skills and behaviour. It seems obvious that to learn, to store and transmit the content of a culture is humanity's most important and distinctive capacity. Nevertheless, that capacity is unlikely to be infinite and it seems probable that some changes in the environment and related human lifestyles will require behaviour which is beyond the capacity of some and conceivably of all.

Thus some students of human ecology, arguing from the dictum of Hippocrates that health is largely a function of the quality of the total environment and of the related lifestyle within it, postulate that if the conditions of life of any animal (including *Homo sapiens*) deviate significantly from those in which the species evolved, signs of maladjustment are likely to occur in the animal. Thus they argue that mankind having evolved in an environment appropriate to a hunter-gatherer lifestyle is likely to show signs of maladjustment, be it physical, mental or emotional ill health, if faced by an environment which deviates significantly from it.

In this oversimplified form, the argument appears to underrate the possibility that changes made by people to the environment itself, and culturally based adaptations of human behaviour, between them could restore a balance initially impaired by deviation from the hunter-gatherer pattern. The hunter-gatherers' competence in their interaction with the environment was itself the outcome, in part at least, of a learned adaptation to it. Subsequent developments in the history of *Homo sapiens* can be seen as a continuous process of mutually stimulated change and adaptation between people and their environment.

Despite our efficiency in learning and in changing the environment, this process is unlikely to proceed without difficulty and tension. There will be occasions when behaviour required by changes in the environment, planned or unintended, cannot be learnt or will be learnt imperfectly. Furthermore, some such changes may prove deleterious even though humankind adapts to them. 'Life in modern cities has become a symbol thus of the fact that people become adapted to starless skies, treeless avenues, shapeless buildings, tasteless bread, joyless celebrations, spiritless pleasures – to a life without reverence for the past, love for the present or hope for the future!' (Dubos 1965: 278). Tension is likely when change is rapid since cultural adaptation is achieved primarily through the education of the young by their elders and by the institutions created by them. Both sources may lag behind the demands on them.

Historically, changes in the environment become increasingly the product of cultural evolution: they are often institutional in character and result from conscious planning. Any limitations on the capacity of *Homo sapiens* to adapt need to be taken into account in the design of such institutional changes. Furthermore, capacity to adapt is unlikely to be uniform through the species. Always some will find the task beyond them and their number is likely to rise with the extent and the rate of change. Many observers see increasing maladjustment in the contemporary human condition.

If account is to be taken of limits to human adaptability and of the needs of those who fall by the wayside, it is more important to understand the physical and psychic needs of members of the species, the characteristics of an environment likely to meet those needs, and the kinds of behaviour which can in fact be learnt. A study of *Homo sapiens* as hunter-gatherer may well contribute to that understanding.

This belief in the relevance of hunter-gatherer experience derives from the following argument. Human beings lived in the hunter-gatherer lifestyle for so long that genetically and culturally they had time to adapt to it and can be presumed to have done so successfully. The adaptation would have been expressed in patterns of behaviour which enabled them to cope with the problems of the lifestyle competently enough to satisfy the physical and psychic needs of survival. In the hunter-gatherer situation adaptation was concentrated in behaviour since the physical, social, cultural and spiritual aspects of the environment were substantially invoked as being constant. Having been confirmed by natural selection the behaviour represented a kind of balance between the needs for survival and the content of the environment.

Whether the transition to other lifestyles – nomadic, pastoral, agricultural, industrial and so on – came because it was believed that they could meet survival needs better, or because pressure of numbers rendered the hunter-gatherer style inadequate, the transition involved changes in both the environment and behaviour. But this mutual adaptation would in due course have achieved a new equilibrium – perhaps at a higher level of success – between the same basic human needs for survival and the environment in its modified form. Both environment and human behaviour would have changed but the needs for survival would be the same. The hunter-gatherer combination of environment and behaviour, therefore, provides a useful starting point for comparisons with other and later lifestyles.

This is not to suggest that the hunter-gatherer lifestyle was superior to other alternatives, but that as the simplest system which links human needs, the environment and human behaviour, it provides a framework within which other lifestyles can be examined and assessed.

AUSTRALIAN ABORIGINAL HUNTER-GATHERERS

In the following section I draw attention to some aspects of that system as they are illustrated in the lifestyle of some Aboriginal Australian communities which still retain many hunter-gatherer characteristics.

The physical environment which surrounded the Aboriginal hunter-gatherer was not only the source of the air, the water, the food and the shelter necessary to survival. It provided also a physical context of which Aborigines were deeply aware, of which their knowledge was profound and with which they experienced an intimate relationship. No one who has had more than a passing contact with Aboriginal Australians within their traditional territory will fail to be conscious of the depth and significance of this relationship.

In the social environments there was a range of social groups: at the base a small group little more than an extended family among whom complex but precise mutual obligations ensured support for one another. Parallel with this 'mutual support' group were others, such as hunting or foraging teams whose members acted together in coordinated effort, or those composed of members more or less kin and who shared common religious and ceremonial traditions. There were also wider tribal or language groups who shared a looser identity and who, from time to time and for specific purposes (usually ceremonial), came together in common activities. Within all of these groups the individual had a known and understood place with related responsibilities and privileges.

113

To the Aborigines both the physical and social environments derived from and were sanctioned by the more fundamental spiritual environment. Both originated in the Dreamtime, when spirit ancestors travelled through the land creating its physical features and the creatures, including people, who were to live within it, and establishing patterns of behaviour governing their relationship with one another, and above all with the spirit ancestors themselves.

These three aspects of the environment – physical, social and spiritual – were for Aborigines recorded and celebrated in the myths, stories, song-cycles, dances, the patterns and designs of their artefacts and decorations and in their ritual and ceremonies. Through these, Aboriginal culture emphasised the integral character of the Aboriginal universe as a part of nature – a place distinctive from, but not inherently more powerful than, that of the animals, or indeed from the spirits whose presence was known but visible only to the few.

A study of the daily life of Aboriginal hunter-gatherers shows that each aspect demanded personal activity and involvement: physical, intellectual and aesthetic. Gould's (1969: 3–26) account of the daily search for food and water demonstrates how much success depended on knowledge, skill and initiative. In the desert, survival required a comprehensive knowledge of the land and its resources, a capacity to read the signs of the presence of other living creatures and to predict their movements, as well as demanding speed of movement and skill in the making and use of weapons. Every day faced Aboriginal men and women with problems frequently having new and unfamiliar components. Gould notes the pride which mastery of these problems justified in the Aborigines. That mastery was the source of a continuing sense of security where changing problems were at the same time a source of stimulus. Indeed, Dubos (1965: 271) argues that: 'Man retains the structures, functions and emotional makeup that emerged in his evolutionary past and it is certain that some form of challenge continues to be necessary for his . . . development and performance.'

The relationship of individuals to their kin and to various groups was also a source of security and stimulus. Each group promised them support in predictable situations and imposed corresponding obligations.

114

The respect of peers and elders depended upon the adequacy with which each person met those obligations.

An Aborigine belonged – with his or her immediate family, with wider kin and age peers, with those who shared totem, with those who shared spiritual and ceremonial life and with those who spoke the same language. Should a person move to another community he or she would at once be placed into corresponding relationships within it. But an individual did not simply belong. In each of these groups each person had a role which differentiated him or her from those others with whom they shared membership: a combination of 'belonging' but also of 'being different' providing the essence of personal identity. Activity is characteristic also of the cultural life of Aboriginal people. The traditional song-cycles, dances, mimes, as well as the sacred and secular ceremonies, involved all in their performance.

This summary may seem to give an idealised picture of Aboriginal society. This is not my intention. There were aspects of the society which were brutal and ruthless. The means by which population growth was limited seem callous and inhuman and the treatment of women was often degrading. Violence in personal and family feuds and in inter-clan strife occurred and was often destructive. Apart from such violence, relations between different tribal groupings were more often marked by suspicion and distrust than by cooperation and friendliness.

Nevertheless, within the small groups, hunter-gatherer lifestyle was characterised by:

- direct involvement in the natural physical environment;
- a high level of activity – physical, intellectual and aesthetic – arising from patterns of behaviour required in social relationships with the different aspects of the total environment;
- involvement in a variety of groups of various sizes in ways which required both identification and differentiation by the performance of a personal role in relation to the group and its corporate affairs;
- a pattern of spiritual beliefs amounting to a conception of the universe which gave coherence and justification to other aspects of a person's lifestyle; and

115

- an active participatory and creative cultural life which recorded and celebrated the integrated physical, social and spiritual aspects of the lifestyle.

These characteristics seemed to provide for each person a balance between a sense of security and of challenge, a personal identity – a combination of belonging and having an individual role, and a sense of contributing to the fulfilment of a cosmic purpose.

This examination of the Aboriginal hunter-gatherer lifestyle suggests a framework by which different lifestyles may be analysed and compared. The environment can be seen as a variety of settings for human activities (see below and Barker 1974). These settings will not be merely physical locations but will also have social and cultural components often including rules or conventions governing the activities performed within them. These activities should provide not merely the material means to survival but also satisfy important psychic needs such as security, challenge, identity and sense of purpose. They call for knowledge and skills which have to be learned and for a capacity to adapt the learned behaviour to deal with problems. Competence based in such capacity will be reflected in a confidence that the problems set by the environment can be coped with.

It may be fruitful to consider how far the more complex and affluent environment of contemporary society can be analysed within the same basic framework so as to highlight the changes which cultural evolution has brought about.

It is necessary at the outset to draw attention to some distinctive characteristics of the contemporary environment. Firstly, it is more complex. It incorporates the accumulated consumers' capital built up over the ages in buildings and structures, in knowledge and skills, in a great diversity of social institutions performing equally varied functions, and in a vast recorded cultural inheritance. All these are capable of being built into settings for human behaviour and, to the extent that men and women have access to them, of offering a range of roles from which a rich and varied experience can be derived. By contrast there was much less diversity in hunter-gatherer society where, apart from a division of function between the sexes, the pursuit of survival imposed the same tasks on all.

116

Secondly, access to the environment is now almost wholly indirect. A hunter-gatherer group, within the limits of its territory, enters into relationship with its environment freely according to the knowledge, skill and wisdom of its members. By contrast contemporary humanity faces barriers to which they must possess the key. The most important of these barriers is property. There is today almost no aspect of the environment, natural or created by mankind, which is not owned by some person or institution. Access to it depends upon the capacity to meet the price set by the owner. In these instances the key to the barrier is wealth or income reflecting the individual's status within the economic system.

Property is a social institution for rationing demand to levels which can be satisfied; that is, for excluding some from the benefits of possession, access, or use of any component of the environment which is scarce. Property has become increasingly important as population has increased and as the potential for man-made components of the environment has been increased by human inventiveness.

Apart from wealth and income there can be other keys to barriers between individuals and the environment. Important among these are the skills and knowledge, less or more specialised, which are required to make effective contact with many of its more complex components. The hunter-gatherer acquired skills from the older generation naturally by progressively increasing involvement in their activities. Contemporary man's skills must be acquired more vicariously – frequently through institutions, access to which is itself rationed either by price or by performance tests.

Such institutions are instances of the environment-behaviour settings to which I have referred. Many of these settings are owned or controlled by authorities – persons or institutions who program their operation so that they serve as instruments of social control – coercing those who act within them to conform to a pattern which the authority sees as conducive to the effective performance of its function (see also Fox 1974: 17–22).

In some instances these settings are controlled in ways which tend to counter the restrictive influence of the wealth and income keys. Thus the State establishes and maintains some whose services are in the nature of public goods – available freely or on concessional terms – or, when rationing is inescapable, bases it upon principles believed to be more humane or egalitarian. Many settings involve groups which might be called voluntary associations. Such associations, formed for whatever purpose, although not wholly free of the constraints of scarcity, can yield important psychic benefit through group activity itself and by expressing a common sense of purpose. These benefits may flow irrespective of the group's purpose: the means may be as important as the end.

These considerations suggest that there will be value in seeing contemporary society as a series of environment-activity settings which offer roles and experience for those who participate in them. They suggest also that the economic system–settings, from which are derived the wealth/income keys giving access to much of the environment, and the educational system (in its broadest sense) from which the skill/knowledge keys are derived, still warrant special attention. Finally, they suggest that experience from voluntary associations may be important and distinctive and less subject than others to the constraints of scarcity.

THE ECONOMIC SYSTEM

In any consideration of the quality of contemporary life the influence of the economic system is dominant and pervasive. Firstly, it has created a substantial part of the existing environment and continues to produce so as to restore what is consumed and to add to or subtract from it. As a result the content of the environment is constantly changing. Secondly, through its rewards in wealth and income, it largely determines access to that content. Thirdly, it is in itself the activity-setting within which men and women will spend more time than in any other, and where the role they perform will largely determine their individual social status.

The claims of the economic system on the environment are comprehensive and potentially universal. The present physical environment incorporates the vast accumulation of productive capital built up in the past – the pastures, tilled fields, the seed, the domesticated animals, roads, vehicles, machinery, factory, shops and offices and the rest.

The social environment incorporates and is shaped by the firms, companies and enterprises which conduct the system, by the cadres of specialists – managers, technologists, accountants – by the institutions, banks and insurance companies, which serve it and by those institutions which train and socialise those who seek employment and opportunity within it and those who consume its products. Even in the cultural and spiritual field it tends to establish and promote values which serve best the efficient operation of the system itself and the interests of those who control it.

The comprehensiveness of these claims means that they will limit the scope for direct experience of the natural environment itself. Environmental resources capable of yielding such experience, for instance, sand beaches and forests, are also potential raw material for the production of other goods – themselves a source of valued experience. As human populations have grown and the demands of the economic system have encroached more strongly on the natural environment, the need to choose between direct experience of it and the goods it could be used to produce has become more urgent. At the margin there is a trade-off relationship between them but the market does not provide an effective mechanism by which preference for direct experience can influence the negotiation of the trade-off.

One consequence of this competitiveness in a world of expanding numbers and technological innovation is the closing off of options for other simpler lifestyles. Thus the enclosures of common land in the Middle Ages of European culture ultimately destroyed peasant lifestyle. Today the intrusion of grazing stock, controlled and feral, and other evidence of market-oriented production, are so changing the fragile environment of the arid lands of central Australia that the hunter-gatherer lifestyle steadily becomes less possible for those Aborigines who may still prefer it. Industrialisation, pressed on by population growth, is in the same way rendering impracticable the varied lifestyles and cultures of Asia, Africa and South America.

The rewards in money terms which the system yields provide a generalised symbolic claim on the owned content of the environment. There are clear advantages in this mechanism. It makes it possible for men and women to choose work in which they are competent or which pleases them, rather than that necessary for survival, and it leaves to individual choice the final real content of the reward itself. Diversity of occupational opportunity and the power to choose between experiences open to consumers are sources of real stimulus and satisfaction. They are perhaps the most valued contributions of the economic system to the quality of contemporary life. Nevertheless, the symbolic role of money can yield results less beneficial. The identification of social status, economic, political and other power with the possession of money lends weight to the influence of those who possess it – enabling them to derive benefits sometimes without their having to sacrifice any of the real wealth of which their money is the symbol.

The choice made possible by rewards in money terms can be made only from among the opportunities offered. I have referred to the fact that the economic system has rendered impracticable some lifestyles widespread in the past. Many who today seek a genuinely different way face great difficulties. Furthermore, as a setting for a large part of the activities of men and women, the system is frequently disappointing. It is to the fortunate, the appropriately talented and, of course, to the wealthy that in the main it offers roles which are secure, stimulating and rewarding. Increasing concern to find new ways of giving job satisfaction to the others is evidence of a growing awareness that, for the majority, experience in the work setting in itself is frequently poor. It is to experiences outside that setting to which most must look for quality in their lifestyles.

I have drawn attention to the importance in Aboriginal society of groups of various sizes, jointly performing important functions, and have emphasised that these groups enable the individual to discover and assert his or her personal identity by the combination of belonging to the group and having within it a distinctive, acknowledged role. In contemporary society also, the work and the consumer context to some extent ensure that similar groups are formed. The work group and the family (the joint consumption group) are, however, unlikely to meet all the individual's psychic needs. There will, therefore, be a natural tendency for him or her to form or join other groups for purposes held in common. These purposes may relate to aspects of the physical, intellectual, cultural or spiritual existence. But independently of the nature of these purposes there seem good reasons to believe that participation in the group will be important to the quality of the individual's lifestyle.

Especially as the processes necessary to gain access to and to consume the means of survival involve less of the individual's time and energy, the activities of such groups will assume increasing importance. In what follows I refer to these groups as voluntary associations to emphasise the fact that they do not necessarily emerge in the pursuit of survival itself but lend a personally distinctive character or quality to that survival. Voluntary associations can include every kind of grouping (outside the work group and the family) from the loving couple, through the changing groups of friends, the street gang, the sporting team, the musical society, to the church and the political party. It can, by a stretch of definition useful for our purposes, perhaps be regarded as including the association with self from which others are excluded where solitude or privacy may be, as it sometimes is, a sought-after objective.

ASSESSMENT

The first task in the assessment of the quality of the lifestyle of an individual or a community is to mobilise coherently the relevant data. This could usefully be done by breaking down the environment into a series of settings for different activities. For many the most important of these would be the work setting, the family home, educational institutions, government agency at various levels and voluntary association. Each of these settings could often usefully be broken down further, and an examination of the individual's allocation of time would show other secondary settings (such as means of transport) which may arise from and be subsidiary to one of the major settings but may develop significant value of its own.

Each of these activity settings could then be considered to identify those of its characteristics which give character to the lifestyle of the individual concerned. Thus in relation to each of them the following groups of questions might be asked:

Physical context
- Does the setting involve contact with the natural environment?

- Does it involve other physical contexts with which the individual can identify?

Activities

- What opportunities does the setting provide for physical, intellectual, aesthetic activities?

Group involvement

- What opportunities does the setting provide for involvement in groups of various sizes?

Identity (role within the group)

- What opportunities for a personal role for the individual do these groups offer?

World view

- Is any activity required by the setting compatible with and does it contribute to the fulfilment of any spiritual, political or other world view the person concerned holds?

The answers to these questions may make it easier to judge not merely how far a particular lifestyle may provide the air, water, food and shelter necessary for the individual's survival, but also how far it may contribute to his or her psychic needs which I have suggested will include security, challenge, involvement, identity, privacy and purpose. It is possible to conceive these data and the related judgements being recorded in a kind of matrix where the various settings are listed vertically and the characteristics of the lifestyle and their contributions to psychic needs horizontally. It is conceivable that the boxes in this matrix could be filled in with values based upon arbitrary scales. These values would reflect the judgement of the individual who made them, and any attempt to combine them into an evaluation of the whole lifestyle would be similarly personal. This does not mean that the compilation of the matrix would be purposeless.

In most real-life situations where a personal choice has to be made most of the settings would be very similar and their characteristics and potential contribution to quality not significantly different. Attention could therefore usually be concentrated on the one or two which are different. If the alternatives are both within the same country, social context, cultural milieu and so on, money incomes may often be accepted as indicative of these main differences. If, however, an individual were offered a position in another country with unfamiliar cultural and religious traditions and a different pattern of working life, the relative money income may well be of lesser importance in assessing the potential offered. In such an instance a matrix of the kind described would at least facilitate the personal assessment which could be called for. It might be difficult to formulate the processes by which a decision would finally be made, but there is no reason to doubt that it would be made and that the process would be substantially rational. However, the use of a matrix, even if agreement were reached about its components, would not go far towards expressing the content of the alternatives in quantitative form.

It has been suggested by Fox (1974: 22–6) that to facilitate such a quantitative expression the concept of income could be extended to comprehend not only those components of experience which can be purchased, but also those components of the natural, social, cultural and other environments which lie outside the market context. It can be argued that, since people do in fact on some occasions choose between purchasable experiences and non-purchasable, the latter must be capable of being expressed also in money calculus. Thus, if an Aboriginal person, in communities I have known, is offered the choice between paid work and unpaid leisure he or she will frequently choose the unpaid leisure. An equivalence at the margin can thus be established between money and the preferred activity-setting combination (for example, joining a hunting expedition).

Thus, the fact that individuals can conceive their environment as a series of settings for various kinds of behaviour provides the basis for their evaluating the experience derived from them. They will be able to judge the content of each setting itself and the role within it which offers probable effectiveness. In the light of that assessment they would be able to arrange possible combinations of settings, roles (and estimates of their effectiveness) in an order of preference and so choose the combination which would maximise the total satisfaction or utility which could be derived from it.

The argument proceeds by pointing out that this capacity to choose between alternative combinations opens the way to quantitative expression of the assessed satisfaction or utility achieved from the chosen combination. This possibility derives from the fact that none of these combinations is entirely free. At the least some sacrifice of time and energy and probably other resources will be required to achieve each of them. Thus it is possible to value quantitatively any one of these possible combinations in terms of its cost – that is, the combination of resources which it is necessary to sacrifice to achieve it.

If time were the only resource which had to be sacrificed to achieve any of the combinations it would be possible for an individual to allocate time between various combinations of settings and related roles, so that the satisfaction at the margin derived from each was equivalent to the extra time necessary to achieve it. The same balancing of benefit and cost at the margin could be carried out in terms of resources other than time – such as effort, the sacrifice of possessions and so on. And of course if money could be used to stand for time, effort, possessions and other resources, the balance at the margin between the use of money and other resources makes conceptually practicable the establishment of money equivalents for such resources. The various combinations of settings and roles, therefore, could be valued in money terms and the aggregate values of those chosen regarded as the total income of the individual concerned.

This argument is ingenious and it is conceivable that an individual facing the problem of choice might find this process of money valuation useful. I believe it could also be useful in the evaluation of environmental intangibles where decisions about the allocation of resources are involved. But it must be doubted whether the total income so assessed would be in any significant sense a measure of the absolute quality of life of the individual concerned. It would rather be another way of expressing the outcome of the choice made between the options open within the limits of the individual's resources. Even less could it be hoped that the aggregation of the total incomes so assessed for all individuals in a community would provide a measure of the quality of life for the community as a whole.

There is a fundamental difficulty in this approach. It ignores the problem of identifying the criteria which would enable the individual to maximise satisfaction from the choice between the possible combinations of settings and related roles. It is the content of these combinations which determines the quality of life. The chosen combination could be assumed to be the optimum only if the chooser were fully informed and infinitely wise. There is ample evidence that humankind's untrained intuitive judgement among increasingly complex and unfamiliar situations provides an inadequate guide to choice. Indeed, interest in the concept of the quality of life reflects the felt need for criteria to guide that judgement and by which to assess the outcome.

In other words, any assessment of the quality of life for an individual will be concerned with the objective capacity of the combinations open to meet his or her physical and psychic needs. If an assessment is to be meaningful, there can be no escape from hypotheses about what those needs are and what kind of characteristics – physical, biological, social and cultural – in such combinations are most likely to meet them.

To assert that such hypotheses are practicable is not to suggest that all members of a community are likely to be best satisfied by the same combination. Indeed, a consideration of the characteristics of possible setting-activity combinations makes clear their infinite diversity and that preferences between them, other things being equal, are likely to be similarly diverse. It may be possible to identify objective minimum standards of air, water, diet and shelter necessary to survival, but these components, assuming they are available, emerge from settings which also meet or fail to meet other physical and psychic human needs. It is with the possible combinations of such settings actually open that we are concerned. The quality of life for a community, therefore, will depend upon the range and diversity of individual lifestyles possible within it and the possession by its members of both the knowledge upon which satisfying choice between them might be based and the keys which would give reality to their choice.

Nevertheless, the matrix as I have described it embodies a chosen set of hypotheses about the considerations relevant to choice. Other hypotheses are possible. To some degree those chosen can be tested. A study of the content of the matrix for individuals whose lifestyles are judged to be clearly successful and unsuccessful respectively could show up differences which might suggest possible reasons for the respective success or failure. Success in this context can perhaps be identified with a confident capacity to cope with the problems presented by the relevant environment-activity settings. In these instances it may be possible to change experimentally the character of the settings concerned in the light of these reasons, and observe whether the effect on the capacity to cope is favourable or unfavourable. This would involve changes not merely in the behaviour of the individual but also in their environmental context.

The matrix, or another based on different hypotheses, may also be used to increase individual and collective understanding of the components which influence the quality of lifestyle. To the extent that it does this, improved use may be possible of the total resources available to the community. Individuals, being better informed, are likely both in market and non-market situations to use total resources more wisely. Furthermore, in their social and political role they will, hopefully, support changes which extend the scope of effective choice for others as well as themselves. The achievement by market and non-market forces of a use of scarce resources which is more efficient in terms of human satisfaction is a purpose to which both economist and ecologist are professionally committed.

Let me conclude by bringing together the main propositions I have advanced:

- The quality of life reflects the capacity of a lifestyle to satisfy humankind's physical and psychic needs.
- Whatever level of material affluence is achieved, psychic needs will remain critical. They include:
  - a balance between security and challenge;
  - a balance between involvement with groups and personal identity;
  - the opportunity for privacy;
  - a sense of continuing purpose; and
  - the opportunity for effective choice.
- These qualities emerge as by-products of the activities of men and women in the environmental settings within which their lives are lived.
- A society which offers its members diversity in such settings, effec-

tive access to them and a real choice among them will best ensure quality in their lives.

- Contemporary industrial society, by its explosive growth in numbers, by its destructive pressure on the natural environment and by the elimination of alternative lifestyles threatens this diversity and the reality of choice.

8

Is Democracy Alive and Well?

Paper presented at the University of Western Australia on their 51st Annual Summer School, January 1979, the 150th anniversary of the establishment of white settlement in Western Australia. Subsequently printed as a Working Paper (10) by the Centre for Resource and Environmental Studies, Australian National University, Canberra, ACT, 1979.

DEMOCRACY IN AUSTRALIA

Australia has been called the Lucky Country. While so many peoples of the world today are deprived and oppressed, we enjoy a relative opulence and freedom worthy of their envy. But to what extent are we aware of our privileged condition and do we strive to practise and protect the democratic rights so enjoyed now and for the future?

There is no doubt that Australians have been given opportunities almost unique to determine their own form of government and to mould it to their heart's desire, and that they are inclined to think of their system as one embodying the essential principles of democracy. It is much less certain that we have used those opportunities wisely and generously, and there are grave doubts about whether our democracy is more than a matter of legal forms and empty processes.

Abraham Lincoln spoke of democracy as government 'of the people, by the people and for the people'. Few would doubt that what we have is government 'of the people'. We have legislative bodies at federal, state and local levels making laws and regulations to control our behaviour and to administer our common affairs. There are also innumerable statutory authorities at all these levels, and some in between, which

128

have authority to conduct activities affecting us all and to whose administrative and executive convenience we must adapt or conform. Daily our community lives become increasingly complex and the need for regulation and control mounts. Year by year the volume of statutes, regulations and by-laws is added to in a rising flood beyond the capacity of any individual to comprehend and recall. With this goes, of course, an army of administrators and officials constituting a bureaucratic machine impinging on our personal lives at every hour of the day. We are certainly a much governed people.

How far, in any significant sense, is this *government carried out by the people* themselves – by those who are themselves governed? During the two years in which I presided over the Royal Commission on Australian Government Administration (Coombs, 1976) I listened to views expressed by people in all parts of Australia, people of widely differing economic and social backgrounds, political convictions and ethnic origin. Among them all, almost without exception, was a conception of government as something distinct and separate from themselves, as an alien 'they' to their own 'we': impersonal, unresponsive, frequently unpredictable and almost always beyond the reach of influence or persuasion. Nowhere did I find, outside the machinery of government itself, any sense of identification with, of sharing in, the processes of government decision-making. Even within that machinery the great majority of those employed saw their personal activities as distinct from, or only obscurely related to, the purposes to which they were collectively directed. They appeared to feel little sense of commitment to or responsibility for those purposes or activities.

In part, this 'we–they' relationship reflected the disparity between the social composition of the community generally and of those who conducted the government's affairs. Educational and other requirements for entry into the bureaucracy meant that many of those encountering officials would face persons whose social background was markedly different from their own and whose attitudes had already been shaped by privilege. An additional factor was the inability of those concerned to confront or even to identify those who actually made decisions. Officers who met members of the community were junior and lacked capacity to make decisions – usually seeing their tasks as

129

simply mobilising information upon which a decision would in due course be made, probably by processes and persons unknown to them. Accordingly they frequently felt it necessary to protect themselves by a cultivated aloofness from distressing and futile involvement in the problem of the person before them. To the client this sense of facing an impenetrable barrier, shielding an anonymous and impersonal authority, was a source of frustration and alienation.

Obviously what we have is not democracy in any strict or literal sense of the word but rather government by representatives – responsible to and elected by adult members of the community – and even more by their officials, neither responsible nor responsive. Someone recently described this as the right to choose, at three-yearly intervals, between alternative tyrannies.

It may be that democracy in a literal sense is possible only in communities small enough for all the members to be gathered together in one place. Perhaps the classic democracy of the Athenian city-state was practicable only because the slaves were excluded from participation in it – reducing the relevant numbers to a level among whom significant oral communication was possible. The town-meeting of the early American colonies, based as it apparently was on early English practice, was another such context. The only examples of such communities I can think of within Australia are those Aboriginal settlements which are still sufficiently isolated to be comparatively immune to government processes, or in the few where the stated policies of the federal government to allow self-management have become reasonably effective. In these communities, decisions are made by consensus reached slowly and by prolonged discussion, not merely within community meetings themselves but also in less formal exchanges between family and extended kin groups and within such groups themselves. Such leisurely procedures may be impracticable in large communities and inapplicable to the urgencies of contemporary affairs.

THE WHITLAM YEARS

But the sharp dichotomy between government and governed, between the 'we' and 'they' of contemporary attitudes, may not be inevitable. Techniques exist by which influence may be exerted on government decision-making and by which those affected may be involved in the administration of programs designed to benefit them or set the context within which their activities are conducted. In the work of the Royal Commission on Australian Government Administration (RCAGA) I was closely involved in the consideration of such techniques. The Whitlam Government had come to office committed to greater community involvement in many aspects of government and there was considerable interest among some groups in giving a more participatory character to the relations between the government and its clients. Commissions and other agencies were established to provide channels through which criticisms, proposals and ideas could flow from interested groups and individuals to ministers and their senior advisers and executives.

The results were exciting but frequently chaotic. A flood of human energy was released and the agencies of government were overwhelmed with information, criticism and plans beyond their capacity to absorb or even to organise coherently. The government's enthusiasm for participation quickly waned. Ministers saw it as an encroachment upon their more traditional personal responsibility for the content management of their portfolios and on their relationships with their official and personal advisers. Advisers too saw it as a rival source of influence. The more established vested interests of the organised power groups, in industry, trade unions, the media, etc, viewed with distrust this encroachment upon their traditional capacity to influence government. In the context of national policies it was urged that these opportunities for participation would tend to be taken up by the most active and articulate rather than those with most to contribute or whose need was greatest. Participation began to be represented by its critics as an invitation to the extravagant, the irrational and those anxious to embarrass the government and the Establishment generally. Even before the end of the Whitlam Government's period in office the appeal of participatory democracy had begun to expire. Since then, one by one, remnants of its influence have disappeared into limbo. The fading of this vision may have been inevitable, but it has left the Australian political scene with little claim to be seen as an example of government *by* the people, and with a community mood of deep cynicism about

the purposes and integrity of those who conduct that government.
But democracy involves more than formal structures of government
and the means by which decisions are made. Defects in its machinery
can be unimportant if its style and spirit are right. To be truly democratic a system of government must be used with the conviction that *all*
its citizens are of equal importance and its policies directed to enabling
them to live lives of dignity and fulfilment and to removing the barriers
of prejudice and poverty which stand in the way of their achieving such
lives. It was, no doubt, with such considerations in mind that Abraham
Lincoln spoke of democracy as government 'for the people'. Any assessment of the quality and health of democracy in any community must
take into account its concern and performance in these matters. A
reasonable measure of that quality and health, therefore, can be found
in the status and welfare of those minority groups which because of
physical, economic, political or social weaknesses lack the capacity to
fend adequately for themselves.

DEMOCRACY AND THE AUSTRALIAN ECONOMY

Before I look at one or two examples of our own performance in
extending justice and compassion towards such groups among us, let
me say a little about the unstated presumptions which have in the past
seemed to underlie our society's approach to these issues. Essentially it
has been presumed that employment for wages can and will continue to
provide the source of rising real incomes and an improving quality of
life for almost all, and that marginal social service support will be
adequate to protect the occasional exception.

During the 1930s it became apparent that the economic system could
not automatically be relied on to provide employment even for all adult
males. Over the following decades governments became increasingly
concerned to sustain levels of total expenditure which would ensure for
business entrepreneurs a context in which they could confidently
expand production and offer employment. These policies, together
with rising productivity of labour flowing from improved organisation
and technology, appeared to justify the presumption that wage employment could provide for generally improving standards.

In recent years governments have encountered a dilemma in the pursuit of these policies. The contexts in which business entrepreneurs had to make decisions were altering. Natural resources – such as oils – basic to many industries were becoming increasingly scarce, and the owners of these resources were in a position to demand a greater share of the proceeds of production. The search for new sources and for substitutes for scarce resources combined with a changing pattern of technology (which included the computerisation of many services) to increase greatly the demand for and the cost of capital. This again encroached upon the earnings of entrepreneurs and restricted their willingness to venture.

In recent years, therefore, governments have put their weight behind the attempts of business entrepreneurs to restore to an acceptable level the share of the proceeds of production flowing to their profits. Since the demands of the resource owners and the providers of capital cannot be evaded their share of profits can be restored only at the expense of that of wage earners. In conditions of full employment, however, the bargaining power of unions would make a significant reduction in that share unlikely. Accordingly, the objective of full employment has apparently, at least for the present, been abandoned and the government has continued to urge a widespread reduction in real wages and to ensure conditions in which wage-earners lack the bargaining power to resist. There are now (1979) more unemployed than at any time since the Great Depression. Young people find entry into the workforce increasingly difficult and the real income of those in employment declines.

These conditions may not be temporary. The basic causes of the change – the growing scarcity of natural resources and the rising demands for capital – seem likely to persist. Technological change, unless it effectively counters these causes, is less likely than in the past to provide the means to reward labour more generously, and the need to constrain the bargaining power of unions may continue to be a predominant influence in economic policies.

We are likely, therefore, to find that the economic system will work to produce more rather than less inequality – to make the rich richer and the poor poorer. Since we continue to rely heavily on overseas capital much of the benefits of that inequality will flow to the owners of that capital abroad while its burdens will fall on those in Australia who must depend on the market for the services they, in their own person, can provide.

These comments on changes which appear to me to be taking place in our economic system may seem to be a digression but they bear upon an assessment of the performance of our democracy in two important ways. Firstly they call into question the reassuring belief that employment for wage or salary can be relied upon, except in marginal instances, to provide a reasonably fair and improving source of real income for practically all who need it. A community in which unemployment is widespread, and in which the level of real wages does not rise, will not merely bear heavily on the weak, the disadvantaged and the unlucky, but will be one in which demands on governments dedicated to government *for* the people will be more insistent and more difficult to satisfy.

Secondly, these changes emphasise the limitations on the powers of governments. The decisions which determine the level of economic activity, the pattern of its production and the effectiveness of its processes are predominantly made by those who exercise other forms of power – or are sometimes dictated by the impersonal logic of the system itself. Yet the capacity of governments to make decisions, even within the areas of social policy, is constrained by the successful operation of that system – so much so that their function is increasingly seen as one of ensuring that success – by their capacity to keep the economic system running smoothly. There are, therefore, serious questions of how far the primacy of the demands of the system will leave scope for changes in the interests of government 'for the people' and of how far all governments, whatever their protestations, may become simply the agents of those in whose hands lies the power to make decisions within the economic system.

DEMOCRACY AND SOCIAL JUSTICE

Let me turn now to our performance, at this stage in our history, in relation to two groups who in justice and compassion are entitled to special concern and whose welfare can be seen as representative of the degree to which our democracy is imbued with those moral values: women and Aboriginal Australians.

It is not my intention to discuss the wide issues raised by feminists in their campaign for equity and opportunity. I want rather to confine my attention to some evidence of more basic injustice – evidence that many women, because of relative physical weakness and economic dependence, are brutally and inhumanly oppressed on a scale of which few people are aware.

During the last few years I have become aware of the existence and the work of a number of women's shelters and of an increasing need and demand for the establishment of more such places of refuge. These shelters are places voluntarily conducted, generally by dedicated women, in which women and children can find sanctuary. Those who go there are frequently the victims of brutal physical abuse, the objects on which drunken husbands work off the disappointments and frustrations of their own lives. Some of these women have been victims of rape. Some are there to protect children from bashing and other physical abuse. Others are simply seeking time and quiet to make decisions about their own and their children's future in a marriage which has failed. Others again are seeking the companionship and support of their fellows who also face the problem of giving meaning to a life currently without purpose or reward. During 1976 there were throughout Australia 15,000 requests for accommodation in these places of sanctuary, by refugees from domestic conflict. Of these, more than 11,000 had to be turned away for lack of space. Only lack of finance and voluntary support prevents the establishment of such centres in cities around Australia. The demand for their services is pressing.

Occasional instances of victimisation are perhaps to be expected in any society, but to read the reports of these refuges, and to become aware of the extent of the pressure on their services and the demand for their establishment in other places, is to come sharply into touch with symptoms of a deep-seated sickness in our society – a sickness which undermines and corrupts the capacity of our democracy to apply the principles of equity and compassion which underlie and justify it.

Even more damaging is the record of white Australians in the occupation and settlement of this land and their treatment of the Aboriginal people who had inhabited and humanised it from end to end for tens of thousands of years. White Australians have been encouraged to think of that occupation as essentially peaceful. It has been presented as a kind of passive infiltration on to the land where Aborigines, depicted as a weaker and inferior kind of human being left behind in the progress of evolution, declined naturally, the inevitable victims of the divine law of survival of the fittest.

Progressively the evidence has piled up that what in fact happened was frequently a ruthless genocide in the face of prolonged and cour-ageous resistance, broken down by the force of a superior technology for the destruction of life. As it became apparent that the land was capable of pasturing sheep and cattle the Aboriginal inhabitants who resisted their entry were subdued ruthlessly. Step by step all land suit-able for the white man's purposes was occupied and Aborigines elimi-nated or beaten into subjection and despair. Only land like the deserts of Central Australia or the inhospitable rocky country or flooded swamps of Arnhem Land, judged then to be of no economic potential, was left. Some of these were set aside and solemnly declared to be reserved 'for Aboriginal use and benefit'. Elsewhere the entry of white settlers and their animals so changed the structure of the environment that the Aborigines' traditional hunter-gatherer lifestyle could not be fully sustained, and surviving Aborigines were often forced into a fringe-dwelling dependence around white communities and home-steads and later around mission and government settlements and insti-tutions (see Rowley 1970).

Even when overt violence was not used the impact of white invasion was invariably destructive. It frequently made Aborigines exiles from their own land and intruders on the land of others. It drastically altered the flora and fauna, eliminating many or making them inaccessible, and replacing indigenous with exotic species whose competitive and preda-tory character made survival of the local species in the same habitat unlikely or impossible. The daily and seasonal pattern of life, the rela-tionship which bound and divided individuals and linked them with the spirit world from which they derived, all tended to be impaired and, with them, the justification and joy of life.

136

It is difficult for us to realise how absolute was the aggression committed against Aborigines by depriving them of the land which a United Kingdom Parliamentary Committee in 1837 acknowledged was 'theirs by plain and sacred right'. Mr Justice Woodward in his report on Aboriginal land rights in 1972 said that Aboriginal possession of the land alone made possible 'the preservation of the spiritual link . . . which gives each Aboriginal his sense of identity and lies at the heart of his spiritual beliefs'. Again Professor W.E.H. Stanner said that in taking the Aborigines' land 'we took what to them meant hearth, home, the source and focus of life and everlastingness of spirit'. In other words, that aggression made impossible and so destroyed an ancient way of life, the social institutions which governed it and a unique culture rich in creativity.

Do not let us imagine that these events were the work of long-dead ancestors for which we can have no responsibility and over which it is purposeless to brood. The process begun in 1788 continues inexorably in our times. It is those lands, previously thought useless to white people, which are now being meticulously prospected and within which mining developments are occurring and are proposed. We have now decided that the reservation of land 'for Aboriginal use and benefit' and even the recognition of Aboriginal title are to be interpreted as subject to the proviso that they must be available to white-controlled enterprises for such purposes as we consider in the 'national interest'. The processes by which this phase of the occupation of Aboriginal land is being completed are justified by Acts of Parliament, are sometimes preceded by some form of negotiation and in some instances bring Aborigines financial rewards, but they are none the less as firmly based upon coercion as their predecessors. The negotiations have not led to truly voluntary agreement and the option to reject is not open to Aborigines. Furthermore, let us not delude ourselves, there is little chance that the impact of the occupations will prove less damaging than those in earlier periods of Australia's history.

Thus in the Northern Territory, in north Queensland and in the north and east of Western Australia, white aggression against Aboriginal territory continues. It forms part of the process, described by

137

Professor C. Rowley (1974), which has sought to eliminate Aboriginal Australians as a distinctive component in Australian society, if not, as in many parts, to destroy them utterly. A truly democratic community would welcome the right of groups of its citizens, with an ancient tradition and sense of common identity, to preserve that identity, as a valuable diversity in its make-up. English-speaking Canadians have come to recognise that they must live with the fact that their French Canadian compatriots will not abandon those elements in their distinctive culture and institutions which they see as an integral part of their society. Likewise we too must learn to live with the fact that Aboriginal Australians have a proud and ancient tradition, a deeply spiritual view of the universe, and social institutions which enabled them to survive in this land for tens of thousands of years.

I believe the time will come when, at long last, the Australian people will acknowledge the wrongs they have done and will conclude a treaty of peace and friendship with Aboriginal Australians which will recognise their rights to land or to compensation for being deprived of it, which will protect their languages, law and culture, and which will acknowledge their right to their own institutions to achieve these purposes. Until this is done the conscience of our people and of the community of nations will continue to deny that there is a just and democratic basis to our society.

DEMOCRACY AND THE ENVIRONMENT

'No man', said John Donne, 'is an island entire unto himself'. The same can be said of mankind. We do not live in isolation, in separateness from, or in opposition to the rest of creation. The web of life consists of an infinity of creatures, of unnumbered species living in a complex of relationships, some symbiotic, some parasitic but always interdependent. We can, if our status in creation seems to us a matter of importance, arrange this complex in a kind of hierarchy and place ourselves at its peak as the crowning achievement in the emerging evolution of life in all its forms. What we cannot do is to isolate ourselves from it and imagine our existence independently of the rest of the hierarchy. Each of these creatures, including humankind, lives in a characteristic natural

138

habitat which is formed by a combination of living and inorganic components. Species from time to time become extinct – usually because changes in the environment render their habitat incapable of sustaining them. We are unique in the diversity of environments which can provide us with a viable habitat and the degree to which we can control and adapt it to our needs. But that capacity is not unlimited and, as mankind becomes increasingly dominant within the web of life, more and more species have found their habitat destroyed by its activities. This in itself threatens our own habitat since we are dependent on other species in ways too complex to fully comprehend. This threat is intensified as population numbers mount and demands for industrial materials grow.

This does not mean that we must accept an unchanging physical environment. Indeed most of the environments within which we live are to a considerable degree man-made. The characteristic mellow countryside of England is largely the product of human activity but it is a countryside which has been developed in harmony not merely with people's needs but with the needs of its other living components; it is essentially sustainable with the uses to which it is put. Even the Australian dry forest landscape, with its open park-like vistas of grassland among the trees, which made it so obviously well adapted to the pasturing of the sheep and cattle of the early settlers, was partly the outcome of the Aboriginal practice of regular small-scale burning of the undergrowth.

But where people modify or change a natural environment they can, by ignoring its character and relationships and the limitations they impose on change, set up processes by which it is destroyed utterly and becomes useless to humans as well as to other species for which it has provided a habitat. The record of the white Australians in this respect is appalling.

Let me give an example. The early settlers in northern New South Wales and Queensland found magnificent forests rich in cedar – a beautiful, easily worked timber. These forests offered a potential resource which would with intelligent management have served the community in perpetuity. In fact, they were exploited so ruthlessly that today the resource does not exist at all and lovers of cedar search antique shops and haunt auction sales to gather the relics of that wasted patrimony. But that is not all. The forests were widely replaced, despite their unsuitable soil, by dairy farms, the great majority of which are now derelict and abandoned. The landscape has been ravaged by erosion and its soil blown and washed away by arid winds and floods made uncontrollable by the destruction of the ground cover. The same is progressively happening to the famous Huon pine – once the pride of Tasmanian forests. (See also Chapter 5.)

All over the world man-made deserts encroach upon productive land. Exploitative land use, ignoring the precepts of soil conservation, takes millions of hectares out of production for pasture and tillage every year. We are unwise to think that we can be immune. Indeed Australians have laid waste rather than developed and nurtured this land. The late Professor Marshall's book *The Great Extermination* (1966) assembles evidence that we have behaved towards it as if, having mined it for what we could quickly take from it, we could return to the lands from which we came and live handsomely on the proceeds, leaving the slow processes of nature to heal the wounds we have inflicted. It is time we learnt that our future may well be threatened unless we can find means to live in harmony with the habitat it provides for us.

DEMOCRACY – ALIVE AND WELL?

Judged, therefore, by our performance in the care and protection of those of our citizens who stand in greatest need of our compassion; in the lack of concern for the fabric of this land we have so lately and so ruthlessly occupied; in our neglect of the rights of other species with whom we share it and those future generations to whom we will leave it, it can scarcely be said that the record of our democracy as government *for* the people is one to excite admiration and respect.

Let us pause, then, among the hosannas we sing in our own praise to take thought for the future: for the judgement which will be made on us when our successors or survivors celebrate our 200th anniversary. [This essay was written in the 150th year of white settlement of Western Australia.] For in this we can, by taking thought, add cubits to our stature. The damage we have done may not be irreparable. We cannot

140

rewrite history but we could share this land with Aboriginal Australians in friendship and fair dealing. Other countries have shown that forests can slowly be restored, the soil replenished and the rivers and streams revitalised. Had we the will we could do much even before 2029.

The chances of such a change of heart may be remote and I am aware that in this review I have been prevailingly pessimistic. I am very conscious that to achieve it will require a rejection of the obsession with material goods and the tendency to regard the environment as no more than a mine to be exploited which have characterised my own generation. Such a rejection, if it is to be made, can be achieved only against the clamour of advertising and the propaganda of the media; only if we choose to live more simply, valuing things of the mind and spirit more and possessions less; only if we turn away from those influences which have made us victims of the cultural cringe and have seduced us into voluntary servitude to the banalities of the American dream.

But I do not wholly despair. I believe that the seeds of the change already are germinating in our society – especially among the young. It is my impression that this is especially evident among the children of those so-called 'New Australians' who in the postwar period sought refuge and a new beginning among us.

This impression has turned my mind to one of the most fascinating episodes in the short history of our people in Australia. In the first settlement of New South Wales the first generation of native-born white Australians – the sons and daughters of convicts, soldiers and settlers – proved to be strangely different from their parents, so much so that they were spoken of as a distinctive group: the currency lads and lasses. They were the first to reject the nostalgic and dependent ties with the Old Country and to identify and see their future wholly with the new. They were the first to see the land with unprejudiced eyes and to find it natural, beautiful and congenial. It was among this generation also that the first signs of a distinctively Australian culture began to emerge – in the songs of protest, in the ballads of the bush and the camp fire tales – a culture orally transmitted, much of which is now lost forever.

Unfortunately, the influence of the currency generations was overlaid by that of successive waves of new arrivals; here not as refugees but hungry to exploit the opportunities the land offered. Nevertheless the

141

currency lads and lasses remained a powerful influence on the formation of Australian society for many decades.

It could be that the changing values of the young of our time are the signs of a new currency generation and that they will mould our future as powerfully as that historic group – perhaps imbuing our history in the next fifty years with a new spirit in which respect and compassion for all humankind and a genuine affection for the land and its creatures will be expressed. It is in this that our hopes must lie.

For there is one thing that can be said of democracy – even of so remote and indirect a kind as our own: that we usually get the kind of government we deserve; that while we remain selfish, acquisitive and aggressive – an 'I'm alright Jack' society – our political masters will by their actions, if not in their words, mirror those values by which we personally live.

Democracy is alive but far from well – morally or spiritually. Its cure must begin in ourselves.

9

Technology, Economic Change and Political Strategy

Originally presented as two separate papers: 'Technology, Income Distribution and the Quality of Life'. Presented as the John Murtagh Macrossan Lecture. University of Queensland, Brisbane, Queensland, March 1980; subsequently published in Search *13(5–6) 1982; and 'Economic Change and Political Strategy'. Presented as the Chamberlain Lecture. University of Western Australia, Perth, WA, December 1980.*

THERE is nothing divinely ordained about the economic system: it is the product of human ingenuity, effort and capacity to organise and, therefore, can properly be questioned, criticised and, if a better alternative exists, rejected. Its justification lies in a conviction that, despite defects, it has provided the populations of western industrialised nations with rising material standards of living over the last two centuries. It has been reasonable to believe that those standards are being increasingly shared by the poorest groups in those societies. It has also seemed reasonable to believe that as its techniques and processes are adopted by other less industrially organised societies, they too will share the experience of the industrial west.

This pattern of beliefs has continued to seem reasonable through changes in the structure of the economic system which, *inter alia*, have meant that the great majority of the population must now depend on employment for wages or salary for their share in what the economic system produces. In oversimplified terms, the system has been justified by the expectation that it would provide employment at increasing real wage levels for those seeking it.

143

From time to time in the system's history confidence in this justification, and the faith in the future which it has provided, have weakened and there has been questioning of whether the system can, or will, continue to fulfil the social expectations of rising affluence, broadening down not merely to the poorest in our own society but also to the beggars on the streets of Calcutta or the Bushmen of the Kalahari Desert. Perhaps even more basic has been the questioning of whether the rising flood of the commodities which the system delivers and the means by which they are produced can properly be equated with an improving quality of life, or can provide a basis for a healthy and happy human society. We seem to be passing through one such period of questioning at the present time.

This questioning appears to derive from changes in the working of the economic system which have been increasingly apparent in recent years and which many fear will become even more influential in the years ahead. I would like to look briefly at the effects of two of those changes: the increasing scarcity of basic resources upon which industrial society depends; and the revolution in the processes of industry brought about by science and technology. I would then like to consider what these effects suggest for the principles which should guide the actions of those who seek by social and political action to improve the lot of those who at present must depend on employment.

SCARCITY AND ECONOMIC CHANGE

In 1972 the Club of Rome reported that at current rates of growth of consumption all the major industrial resources – such as fossil fuels, minerals and timber – could be exhausted in the lifetime of those now living. They argued that the pressure of mounting population on agricultural and other land, on water and other finite resources, set limits to the growth of human society and its economic system, and that we were already pressing on those limits.

Most contemporary economists have rejected the prospects of exhaustion. They point to the capacity of the price mechanism to ration the use of resources and to stimulate the development of substitutes by greater use of scientific and technological innovation. Personally I see these capacities as no more than qualifications of the essential truth that because the world's resources are exhaustible, unlimited growth is as much a contradiction of natural law as perpetual motion.

It is, however, the more immediate effects of scarcity which I wish to emphasise – its effects on the distribution of the final product of productive enterprise between those engaged in it and on the general level of prices. Elsewhere in these papers I have used evidence – the 1973 world oil crisis and the industrial revolution in England – to argue that increasing scarcity brings about a redistribution of wealth and of income and, that as scarcities become more widespread and more acute, redistribution will be more significant. This redistribution obviously will favour those who own the natural resources. Its effects on others engaged in production need further consideration.

It is useful in that consideration to envisage the problem facing the entrepreneur – the person responsible for organising production – of bringing together the various factors involved. The entrepreneur will have to make increased payments to those who provide the materials and fuels which are affected by scarcities. Unless he is in a sufficiently monopolistic position to be able to pass on to consumers the whole of those increases, he will be concerned to protect his own share at the expense of others involved. These others are primarily those who provide the financial capital and the labour he employs.

The entrepreneur's chances of squeezing the return to those who provide capital are slender. Competition for capital in finance markets is strong. In conditions of scarcity the production of natural resources is pushed increasingly into the use of less and less suitable and accessible sources. With rapidly changing technology, the trend is generally for more capital-intensive methods to be used, so intensifying the demand for capital. The entrepreneur, therefore, will be able to avoid a reduction in his own share of the product only by squeezing that of his employees. A reduction in unit labour costs can be achieved by increasing the scale of output or by using less labour-intensive methods. Entrepreneurs are likely to be pushed into technological change for this purpose. This will increase dependence on those who supply capital but may make it possible to increase output or otherwise reduce labour costs.

In this process the bargaining power of an entrepreneur's employees is weak unless they, or some part of them, possess monopolistic advantages in skills or a critical role in the productive process which enables them to extract a rent-like share in the final output. But technological change affects the bargaining power of wage and salary earners, both through the demand for labour within particular industries and in the economy generally, as well as in the nature of the work processes – the skills required and the structure of the work force which performs them.

Before examining the effects of technological change it is necessary to consider the effect of increasing scarcities, and the changes in wealth and income they bring about, on the structure of prices. It is obvious that as basic resources such as fuel and minerals become more scarce their prices will rise, driving up the costs of all industries which use them. Unless other costs can be cut the prices of the goods produced by those industries will rise. In such a situation a rise in the level of prices generally – that is, inflation – can be avoided only *if other prices fall*. If they do not fall the owners of the scarce resources can extract the benefit which their monopolistic position confers on them only by raising their prices still further. In other words, a cumulative process of increasing prices is established. The economist looks to more rapid technological change and to a reduction in the level of real wages to check this cumulative inflationary trend and it is towards them that the logic of the market-place points.

It is not easy to be certain about who gains and loses from inflation. Owners of existing physical assets and those with debts, especially with fixed-interest charges, seem to benefit. Those who live on fixed incomes clearly lose as generally do those who, at intervals, have to negotiate for increases to match the rising prices and who find that those increases, when achieved, have moved them to higher tax brackets and that prices have already risen further. But it is certain that those who are economically weak, ignorant, unlucky or in other ways unable to protect themselves are more likely to suffer than the powerful and the well informed. Certainly, the bargaining power of labour is weakened by the difficulties and delays in negotiation, by any reduction in the demand for labour brought about by new technology and by government policies designed to reduce the general level of demand as a check to inflation.

TECHNOLOGY AND ECONOMIC CHANGE

Technological change – at least those forms of it which affect the demand for labour – is, in essence, the application and working out of the principle of division of labour. By breaking down a particular form of production into separate processes it becomes possible to entrust each stage to specialised workers, who by natural aptitude or repetition become much more efficient in it than one responsible for the whole task of production. This breaking down facilitates the design of tools and equipment which take further the increase in the output each worker can achieve. In due course it frequently becomes possible to design machines which perform the various processes more rapidly and uniformly than the most skilful worker. This greatly increased potential leads to the growth of the size of the productive unit with many economies of scale. With that growth in size the role of organisation and management becomes increasingly important. It is only at the level of management that the whole productive process is conceptualised, the interrelations of its component parts understood, and where effective decisions can be made.

With these changes have gone corresponding changes in the structure of the workforce. The craftspeople capable of performing the whole of a productive process give way to process workers performing part of it only and supervised by a foreman in accordance with an overall plan. But the task of the foreman is itself, in due course, subject to change by the application of the same division of labour. The control of the process workers is achieved largely by gearing their work to the machine and by mechanical recording devices feeding their results up to the management level. Control becomes more remote and impersonal. As mechanisation followed on division of labour, so the number of process workers required declined.

To some extent this decline was offset by increases in the numbers engaged as support for management. Decision-making required information, and managers built up staffs to mobilise, codify and present such information. Many of those who formed these staffs were employed in the offices rather than in the factories or productive units of the firms concerned, and some became members of the staffs of separate service agencies providing information and other services to managers also of other firms.

Another offset to the decline in employment in the productive activities came in the expansion of the marketing aspect of management. The increased output of the individual firm necessary to maximise the economies of scale meant a separation of production from its market which was not merely larger but also more distant and dispersed. To maintain supplies to it, to ensure service where the products required it, to persuade all components of the market to accept the uniform product, to feed back to management its responses, all involved tasks both more complex and more difficult, and more and more workers became involved in them.

It was in management services and in marketing that occupational changes in the structure of the workforce became most evident and where the main offsets occurred to the loss of jobs in the physical productive process. These occupational changes were supplemented by the production of new goods and services. The proceeds of the sales of the item produced by these innovative processes emerged as income for those engaged. The decline in the incomes of workers in the productive part of the process was offset, in part at least, by increased payments to those engaged in servicing management and in marketing both within the firm and in independent agencies. There was, too, the growth in payments to the owners of materials, capital, equipment, processes, know-how and special skills made necessary by the increased scale and complexity of the new forms of production. Finally, of course, there were the increased profit incomes the prospect of which had stimulated and justified the technological changes. The expenditure of the incomes increased by these higher payments was reflected in increased demand for goods and services, sometimes satisfied by new products creating new opportunities for profit and for employment.

It is to this increased demand from the incomes of those who benefit directly from technological change that economists look to bridge the gap in employment opportunities opened by the reduction in the

148

demand for labour which is its immediate effect. It is an axiom of economic theory that the income from any form of productive activity will, given time for adjustment and appropriate changes in relative prices, produce effective demand for goods and services to absorb all productive resources available including labour. It was this axiom which Keynes disputed in his General Theory. He pointed out that most income earners saved a proportion of their income – that they had a 'propensity to save' as well as a 'propensity to consume'. These propensities were related to their incomes but not to income alone and it was only the income spent on consumption of goods and services which could be expected necessarily to be reflected in the demand for productive resources as the axiom required. The resources freed by decisions to save income earned were brought into production by decisions to create capital assets – for the production of additional commodities or for direct enjoyment. Such decisions were made substantially independently of the decisions to save which freed the relevant resources and the capital market did not necessarily bring them into balance. Keynes argued, therefore, that the system could be in equilibrium at a level of expenditure on capital assets creation insufficient to employ the resources, including labour, which were available. Whether the incomes increased by technological change will be expressed in increased demand for goods and services on a scale adequate to employ the labour and other resources it renders idle initially may well depend, therefore, on the effect of the changed distribution of income on the propensities to consume and to save and on the desire to create new capital assets.

Another possible qualification of the job-creating capacity of expenditure from incomes increased by technological change may derive from the fact that technological change is not simply a number of discrete instances of change but a continuous process. Even if one such change, however large, could be expected in due course to be followed by increased incomes on a sufficient scale to produce the market demand to absorb the released resources, this could not necessarily be expected to occur if that technological change were merely one of a series following from a continuous process. If the rate of change resulting from that process were sufficiently rapid it might require a rate of

149

adjustment beyond the capacity of the system. The result, in such circumstances, would presumably be a persistent lag in the emergence of
new demand reflected in unused resources of changing composition.
The volume of these unused resources could be expected to fluctuate
with changes in the rate of technological change.

TECHNOLOGICAL CHANGE AND THE WORKFORCE

It is for these reasons that I think it important to consider the probable
effects of technological change on the distribution of income. Those
effects will bear heavily upon the capacity of the economic system to
adapt to that change and the capacity of those dependent on wage employment to share in its benefits. I will return to this issue, but first I
would like to consider briefly the effects of technological change on the
nature and distribution of skills in the workforce and its effects on the
quality of the work experience. I do this both because the work experience itself represents a major part of the quality of life of those engaged
in it and because the skills and aptitudes are the marketable assets of
workers – the demand for which in production will affect their capacity
to bargain in the labour market.

The outstanding effect of the application of the principle of division
of labour and technology is its polarisation of those engaged in production. In pre-industrial production, whether on the farms or in the
craft-based activities of townspeople, those engaged, whether farmers
or labourers, whether master craftsmen, journeymen or apprentices,
built up from experience or formal training an understanding of and
skills relevant to the whole process. Industrial production, in contrast,
has become not merely a complex social process but also one whose
comprehension and management demands scientific, technical and
engineering knowledge. This knowledge is not concentrated in the
proprietor or top manager but is dispersed through the administrative
and executive staff organisations associated with management. Only at
the focus of policy formation and decision is it brought together and
used vicariously by decision-makers. What is left to workers at the production level is a specific dexterity in a limited task which is usually

acquired with a few weeks or months experience and the need for which may disappear with further change. The relevance of that task to the total process can and often does remain obscure to those performing it. There can be little doubt that intellectually and emotionally the work experience of these contemporary workers is impoverished when compared with that of their craftsmen or farmer predecessors.

The scale and complexity of industrial production, however, creates the need for management, if it is to make the most effective use of this labour and existing technology, to be supported by a diverse body of employees providing information, special knowledge and skills. Many of the services these supporting staff provide call for specialised training and experience. In almost all of them there has been a need for educational standards possible only to those who have attended schools, colleges and universities for long periods. For these reasons and because of their association with the proprietorial and managerial function, the jobs associated with providing these services have possessed a social cachet not open to the process worker. It has been the great increase in the number of these management supporting roles which has lent later industrial society its characteristic social form and has produced the white-collar 'company people', who feel no community of interest with the process workers but identify with and accept the values of proprietors and top managers.

Increasingly, however, the roles of those providing management support have themselves become the subject of the same process which had polarised those of the 'blue-collar' workers. The same breakdown of the tasks they perform, the design of tools and equipment capable of performing them more rapidly and uniformly, and the application of science and sophisticated technology to these processes are enabling these roles to be performed with fewer people in organisations (within or outside the producing firm) which are microcosms of those firms. In such organisations only the top management comprehends and directs the whole process with the support of specialists in sections of it and others providing information and expertise. As this polarisation occurs, the 'monopoly' advantage conferred by their capacity to fill the management support role weakens. The role is performed increasingly by machines and by persons with no more than a specific dexterity, readily acquired. Such persons progressively are rewarded at levels more closely comparable with the industrial process worker. Indeed, what is now happening with the extension of technological change into the field of management support occupations can perhaps be described as making a proletariat of white-collar workers.

Two interesting consequences derive from this process. The first is that the level of education which in recent years has been demanded of entrants into these management support occupations is now increasingly seen to be largely irrelevant to their performance, except for the very few. Indeed, it is likely to be seen as a nuisance to employers, establishing expectations both as to income and work style which they will find unnecessary and so be unwilling to provide. The recent change of attitude among industrial and political leaders towards institutions of higher learning may well reflect this development. The second consequence is that the work experience of the white-collar worker, which until recently has been markedly superior to the blue-collar equivalent, is losing some of its privileged character. Closeness to the point of decision, the sense of providing information or knowledge essential to those decisions, the sense of identity with top management, added to the capacity to demand an income embodying a margin for their special capacities, gave white-collar workers a work experience more satisfying and fulfilling. With the polarisation now occurring, many, perhaps most, are more likely to share the impersonal, apparently purposeless work experience of the industrial process worker. However, the few who, despite these changes, remain essential to management acquire even greater bargaining power. Their monopoly position is strengthened.

Whether technological change can produce other consequences which will offset or more than offset the increasing polarisation of the workforce depends on: whether the labour and other resources released as a result of technological change can be employed in the production of other goods and services, thus making possible a larger total product; and whether those dependent on employment for wages or salaries will be able to share in that product to a degree which will satisfy social expectations.

TECHNOLOGICAL CHANGE AND INCOME
DISTRIBUTION

As I have said earlier, the answer to these questions will turn, in part at least, upon how the increased sales revenue of those firms benefiting from technological change is distributed as income to those involved, directly or indirectly and the effect of that distribution on the propensity to consume or to save of those who receive it.

It would be valuable in considering this question if a breakdown of sales revenue into payments to those who had been involved were available for some firms before and after a significant technological innovation. It was hoped that the Myers inquiry into technological change (1980) would have carried out a series of case studies of such firms, but in the absence of such information one can only speculate. To conduct such studies would be a useful research project.

Thus one can assume that the fundamental change is that proportionately less of sales revenue is spent on labour and that finally there is a larger proportionate return in profit to the entrepreneur – the proprietor(s) of the firm. But there will be some components to which increased payments must be made before the entrepreneur's profit can be determined. There will, of course, be payments to producers of raw materials and power and to those who provide transport and similar services. Presumably these will be larger in absolute terms, but whether they are proportionately larger will depend upon whether the technological change is primarily labour-saving or whether it enables other economies. Most labour-saving changes involve greater reliance on machinery and equipment and, therefore, increase the need for capital and the proportionate share of the total proceeds flowing to those who provide it. Important also will be the cost of access to the new technology itself.

Contemporary new technology is characteristically based upon research and development programs conducted in universities and similar research institutes or, recently more importantly, within large corporations. Where the initial research has been done in a public institution, such as a university, the results have increasingly been shared with established corporations as the institution's best hope of deriving reasonable reward for their share in the innovation. Ownership of the innovation, even when protected by patent, is rarely sufficient. Few innovators within research establishments have the knowledge or the resources to carry through the pilot model stage, mount an expensive production program and advertise and sell the resulting product. Consequently, technological innovations today are characteristically the property of large corporations. Smaller corporations find it more economical to buy rights to use these innovations under licence for an appropriate royalty or fee. For most firms, therefore, technological innovation will require increased payments to owners of technology for access to it and to the know-how required to make use of it.

These payments will not be the end of such new expenditures. Sophisticated technological processes frequently require the services of technicians and consultants of various kinds, each with a capacity to command a component in their remuneration for special knowledge. Indeed, while those who supply the 'support for management' function tend, with recent technological developments, to be greatly reduced in number, those who remain are often in a strongly monopolistic position because of the dependence of the whole process on them.

There are, I think, certain general conclusions which can be drawn about this pattern of outlays of an enterprise introducing technological innovation. Such a firm will characteristically:

- pay more to owners - owners of rights to technology, of capital, or natural resources;
- pay more to other corporations and less to persons;
- pay more to a small number of persons with special knowledge, skill or organising capacity who in some way are indispensable;
- pay more to persons or firms outside the enterprise and less to those actually engaged in it; and
- in Australia pay more to persons and firms abroad and less to those in Australia.

The shift of income in favour of owners of capital, of scarce resources, of technology, etc, and that in favour of corporations, means a shift in favour of the already wealthy. It is the expression in income terms of the polarisation of those engaged in production to which I have referred. Such a shift is likely to reduce the community's 'propensity to consume' and to increase the 'propensity to save' and so limit the increase in the volume of consumer spending from which new employment opportunities might flow. This is even more likely to be true of income which goes to corporations which generally retain a much larger proportion of their earnings for capital purposes than do individuals. How far this increased allocation to savings of the income of corporations and the wealthy can help offset the immediate reduction in the demand for labour produced by technological change will depend on the scope which exists for the profitable creation of capital assets.

This dependence will be augmented by two other aspects of the changed distribution. An increase in the incomes of the wealthy, even if it is spent, may well be devoted to the purchase of existing assets rather than of products newly created. Furthermore, since an increasing proportion of the productive agents are owned or controlled from abroad, it follows that the income and expenditure arising from payments to their owners will occur in economies other than our own and most stimulus to employment will occur there also.

Thus the major distributional effect of technological change, certainly in a context of increasingly scarce natural resources, is to shift income towards those most likely to save and in the best position to invest in the creation of new capital assets. How far this shift will lead to increased employment opportunities depends on how far profitable opportunities exist for the creation of such assets and on the alternative uses to which the saved income can be directed. The most favourable circumstance for the creation of new employment opportunities would be those in which (perhaps as a result of technological change itself) new products likely to be widely demanded by consumers had been developed. The introduction of television as an almost universal component in domestic life is an example of such a development in the past.

In their absence those who make decisions about the use of savings (and especially corporate funds) are likely to turn to expenditure which will reduce their payments to others: labour-saving devices, and the development of alternative sources of, or substitutes for, scarce resources over which others exercise 'exclusive power'. Where such opportunities do not exist or are inadequate, savings are likely to be used to acquire from others the 'exclusive power' over productive resources or the opportunity to exploit monopolistic advantage of some other sort. The flush of interest in 'takeovers' in recent years suggests that, to many who command investable surpluses, this seems the most fruitful use to which they can at present be put. Such transactions do little to increase productive capacity or to provide employment opportunities. They serve primarily to intensify the concentration of ownership and the wealth and income which goes with it.

TECHNOLOGY AND RESOURCES IN AUSTRALIA

Two components of the contemporary Australian scene appear likely to intensify these adverse prospects for new job creation. Australia is potentially a major source of increasingly scarce energy and minerals for the world economy. The best prospects for the profitable investment of financial surpluses, therefore, are in the development of these resources for export production – coal, uranium, iron ore, timber, etc. The most profitable exploitation of these resources requires that they be worked on a huge scale by highly capital-intensive methods. The finance required by such methods is almost invariably beyond the capacity of Australian enterprise to provide or that of the Australian capital market to mobilise. Furthermore, experience in such massive exploitation exists predominantly in the great multinational mining corporations of the world. The Australian enterprises, therefore, are usually owned or dominated by such corporations.

These mining enterprises use little labour in relation to the value of the output, although what is used tends to be highly paid by Australian standards. Investment in them, therefore, does little to counter the lag in job creation which the steady application of new technology to existing production tends to create. Furthermore, the enterprises are essentially part of the world economy. The later stages of the processes in which the fuels and raw materials are employed occur mainly in other economies. Where a choice can be exercised it will be in the interest of the enterprise to direct labour-intensive phases of those processes to

economies where labour costs and the attitude of trade union nego-
tiators are thought to be most favourable to management.

A related component in the Australian scene of these major developments in basic resource exploitation is their effect on the structure of
the Australian economy as part of that of the world as a whole. Those
developments offer the opportunity to use capital and entrepreneurial
capacity to earn a large part of our total income from exports to the
world market and to use the proceeds to buy imports of manufactured
goods from international sources more cheaply than they can be produced here. There are many economists who believe, and official
reports which support the view, that official policies should be directed
to expediting these structural changes. The impact of those changes on
many Australian manufacturing industries which must compete either
on world markets or with imports within Australia require, these economists argue, that they be made more competitive by more rapid
technological change and/or by a reduction in real wages.

THE CHANGING ECONOMIC SYSTEM

Let me try to bring together the judgements it is possible to make about
the implications for wage and salary earners of the two dominant components of change in the contemporary economic system; that is, the
increasing scarcity of basic resources and the increasingly rapid rate of
technological change.

- Both components are shifting the distribution of wealth and
  income in favour of the owners of scarce resources, or capital, and
  of technology.
- This shift is the result of increased prices for the use of the
  resources they own and of the goods in which they are embodied.
  Unless other prices fall the increase in these prices will bring about
  a general rise in prices; that is, a tendency to inflation.
- With this shift goes a growing concentration of knowledge, skill,
  authority and power in the hands of the few and a polarisation
  from them of the rest of those engaged.
- Technological change usually produces an automatic reduction of
  employment in the firms where it is introduced and a decline in the

157

skills, status and job satisfaction of wage and salary earners. This decline increasingly involves also those who have in the past provided support for management and who have generally enjoyed a relatively privileged position.

- The shift of income towards owners usually benefits corporations more than persons, those outside the enterprise more than those in it, and often those outside the country concerned rather than those in it.

- Whether the greater income flowing to those who benefit as owners of resources or technology will show itself in newly created jobs will depend on what proportion of the higher income is saved and whether profitable opportunities exist for new investment. (In present circumstances those with financial surplus show more interest in purchasing existing property rights or in speeding up the rate of technological change than in widening employment opportunities.)

- All of these judgements suggest that the bargaining power of those Australians who are dependent on employment for wage or salary is likely to be weakened. The unemployment and declining real incomes many of them have experienced in recent years appear likely to continue.

This is a pessimistic assessment and many will reject it. I hope it proves wrong but, to the extent that it is correct, it seems to call for changes in political and industrial strategy which at present continues to be based upon an expectation that the industrial system is capable of producing a steadily increasing total volume of goods, and that the bargaining power of organised labour will enable it to command an increasing share of it.

PRINCIPLES FOR A POLITICAL STRATEGY

What those changes should be raises challenging issues and demands creative thought from those who share the view expressed by Chifley that society has a responsibility to protect those whose need is greatest. What I have to say about this issue is designed to promote such thought. A more realistic strategy might be directed to:

- redistributing the increasing share of the total product which will go to owners of scarce resources and of technology;
- increasing that part of real income which comes from individual and group effort outside the market economy;
- reducing the wasteful consumption of goods not necessary to, or excessive for, the real health and welfare of the community – particularly those which are extravagant in the use of energy; and
- using labour otherwise likely to be unemployed for the protection and improvement of the physical and social environment in rural and urban contexts.

Such a strategy would, I believe, reduce the dependence of wage and salary earners on income from industrial employment and counter the tendency for real incomes of wage earners to decline.

The opportunity to take at least a first step in this direction exists in the fact that the increasing scarcity of natural resources provides 'rent-like' profits to those who own those resources. John Stuart Mill, in discussing the privileged position of English landlords, drew attention to the fact that it was only 'the arrangements of society' which conferred these privileges on them. He went on to assert that the monopoly accruing to those who exercised this absolute power over the use of those resources could not be prevented, but that it could be held in trust for the benefit of the community.

In fact in Australia our governments are so desperate to enable multi-national companies to exploit the natural resources over which 'the arrangements' of our society have given those governments power that they make them available on terms which frequently are ludicrously unrelated to the profits which can be extracted from their use. Most governments in Australia go even further. They often use the tax-payers' money to provide for these exploiting companies the infra-structure in transport and port facilities upon which their activities depend and which frequently add little to the facilities used by the community generally.

It is now widely agreed among economists that there is a strong case for a resources tax which falls upon the excess profits of those into whose hands the community's supplies of basic resources have been given to develop. There is a variety of forms which such a tax could take. Alternatively, graduated royalties could be devised.

I suggest that the proceeds of such levies should be treated differently from ordinary tax revenues. They would represent a charge made by the community for the use of wasting capital assets from which all should benefit. If they are used simply to finance government expenditure in the usual way they would make possible the reduction of taxes which would otherwise have to be paid. Such reductions would primarily benefit the wealthy and the high income earners. It would be relatively simple to add an equal share of these levies to the taxable income of everyone in the community so that those below the exemption line would receive a full net addition to their after-tax income, while those at the other end of the income scale would benefit only marginally.

In addition to the yield of the resources tax there are other incomes accruing directly to the government which should logically be dealt with in the same way. The Commonwealth Government is the owner on behalf of the community of a number of profit-earning enterprises and other income-yielding assets. At present the annual return from these goes direct to consolidated revenue and is used as if it were derived from taxation. It therefore benefits those in the high tax brackets more than proportionately. It would be logical for it to be distributed equally and become subject to taxation at the rate appropriate to the individual's total income.

Personally I believe that the proceeds of death duties, inheritance taxes, etc, and all taxes which fall on capital also should be dealt with separately from taxes on income. They too should be held in trust for the community. They should be paid to a capital fund which represented the 'common wealth' of the community and only the income from it should be distributed or used. Indeed, except for the family home, personal possessions and, with some limits, genuine family-operated farms and other individually operated enterprises, I believe all corporate and financial assets should revert to the community on the death of their owner – with the proviso that a person should have the right to bequeath the income from it as a life interest to his or her heirs.

In this way there would accumulate a body of income-earning assets which would, to use Mill's language, 'be held and used in trust for the community'. Every member of the community would in effect have a 'rentier' interest in that body of assets and would receive a regular 'dividend' from its income.

This proposal is a form of 'minimum income'. It differs, however, in that so far from being a kind of 'welfare' receipt it would be an entitlement deriving from the citizen's right to share in the 'common wealth' of the community.

But it is not only from such a governmentally organised redistribution of wealth and income that greater independence of employment can be derived. If one looks at communities around the world and attempts to assess the quality of life enjoyed by their members it becomes apparent that their relative status is not accurately indicated by their money income adjusted for price differences. I recently saw a report of an attempt to apply very simple tests of that quality of life to various populations. One surprising outcome was that Sri Lanka, a country with low money income per head, ranked very high in standards of health – physical and psychic – in literacy and other measures of culture and in other indicators of well-being.

The reasons for this appear to lie in the characteristic pattern of life and the resources which are available to their people from sources other than the market economy. In Sri Lanka, outside one or two cities, communities are small. There is land, water and a genial climate so that self-sufficiency gardening is easy. There is a strong tradition of mutual help and the community provides most health and social services from within its own membership. The Buddhist monks are the teachers and the guardians of a rich cultural heritage shared by all.

There is little doubt that under the pressure of advertising we have come to depend unnecessarily on the commodities of the market economy and to identify welfare excessively with their possession and consumption. Interest in the search for various 'alternative' lifestyles suggests that many are seeking ways of life which are simpler, less materialist and based more on sharing and mutual care within smaller groups. These lifestyles may not be practicable for people generally, and many are repelled by the more extravagant aspects of the 'alter-

161

native' movement. Nevertheless, there is good reason to believe that there is scope to enhance the non-market components in our individual and community lives. Within these, the narrowness of specialisation and the polarisation of the few who exercise power from the many whom they manage impose fewer constraints. Within them, too, we can be freer of both big business and big government. At present the development of these non-market activities is inhibited by difficulties of designing appropriate forms for them and by hostility and suspicion in both government and industrial quarters. This hostility seems to be unwarranted. On the contrary, there may be more scope for additions to human welfare from such activities than would be provided by exclusive reliance on the employment offered by the market economy. They could be stimulated by more systematic study of their possibilities and by more enlightened administration of both taxation laws and of social services.

As the constraints of scarcity become sharper it will become more urgent to differentiate between the use of resources to meet genuine human needs and those demands justified only by affluence. To this end, I believe we must resort to differential pricing. For water, electricity, petrol and other important components in the cost of living using exhaustible resources, it would be possible to provide a basic per capita quota at a price designed to limit the burden of scarcity on needs and to impose sharply graduated price increases for supplies above that level.

There is also no doubt that advertising stimulates the worst excesses of the consumer society. It is quite unjustified to regard as a cost expenditure on advertising designed to create or defend a monopolistic advantage for a particular product or brand. Present advertising expenditure is clearly excessive for simply informing the consumer of what is available. It would be simple to set a maximum percentage for advertising expenditure as a cost admissible for taxation. Expenses in excess of this should be regarded as expenditure of profits or of capital and taxes should be assessed on income before those expenses have been met.

These measures to reduce the pressure of consumption on scarce resources could be supplemented by directing taxation at expenditure

162

rather than at income. I do not mean indirect or value added taxes which are usually designed to shift the burden of taxation more on to lower and middle incomes. I mean a graduated percentage tax which falls on funds coming to the taxpayer from both income and the sale of assets, but allowing substantial rebates for the saving and investment of those funds in financial assets. Such a tax which encouraged saving would encourage the better-off to perform the function of accumulating capital which classical economists saw as the prime justification for the existence of the profit-maker, and would encourage all to be the more sceptical of the claims of the advertiser. Furthermore a higher level of personal and corporate saving would help keep interest rates within more reasonable limits and reduce the need to finance imports by selling off the nation's capital assets.

The measures I have outlined to redistribute income and to encourage non-market productive activities would contribute to some improvement in employment prospects as well as reducing the hardships of unemployment. Added expenditure by wage and salary earners and the unemployed, made possible by that redistribution, would be more likely to create new jobs than expenditure by the owners of scarce resources and of sophisticated technology. High levels of savings and lower interest would reduce the cost of home ownership or rental. But it would be idle to suggest that the ideas I have proposed would return us to a world of full employment and of stable prices.

The effects of increasing scarcity – especially of energy resources – on prices may be moderated but I see no way in which they can be eliminated. It is for this reason that I have made proposals for income redistribution to help mitigate the effects of higher prices on those least able to bear them the central propositions of the strategy I have outlined.

Similarly, while I reject the current monetarist conviction that nothing can be done about unemployment until inflation is brought under control, I am suspicious of plans to stimulate the private sector by an indiscriminate expansion of government spending or by reductions in taxation. Disciplined budgetary policy is a vital component in economic management.

Nevertheless, the community cannot properly ignore the waste and inequities associated with widespread and continuing unemployment. The opportunity to deal with this problem sanely and with generally beneficial results exists in two special areas. Firstly, it is obvious that the rising cost of energy and the long-term threat to energy resources makes a reduction in the use of energy a high priority. Not merely will such a reduction economise on fuel resources but it will also reduce significantly the capital investment required in energy production. A two-level pricing system to which I have referred would contribute to such a reduction but more is possible. In particular, a diversion to solar energy could make a major contribution to reducing the pressure on oil, coal and other exhaustible sources and help constrain the increase in their prices. Similarly, for purposes such as space heating and air conditioning, major economies can be achieved by better building design and insulation. It is noteworthy that both the development of solar energy, with its concentration on smaller dispersed units, and the installation of improved insulation, are much more labour-intensive than extensions of traditional ways of generating energy. It would make sense, therefore, for the government to divert resources from the expansion of energy-generating plants to the development of solar energy and to support the modification of buildings to reduce power consumption. Some diversion of agricultural effort to the production of energy from crops may contribute to the same ends, provided that it would be achieved without loss of food production and without environmental damage.

It is in relation to the environment that the need and the opportunity exist to extend the range of employment opportunity. Today, the impact of people's ostensibly productive activity is, almost without exception, destructive. For example, forests are laid waste for wood chips for the newspapers of the world; they are eaten into and endangered by miners; and disease is spread among them wherever man intrudes. The threat is not to the forests alone – for they are in Australia both the source and the protector of the water on which human life and activity depends.

We could recover and restore the catchments of those rivers which are already salt; we could protect those remaining not yet saline from a like fate. We could stop the pollution of the coastline with the garbage of the miners and the wastes of the cities. We could in our cities and towns and in their suburbs create, where it does not already exist, a context within which all, however poor in money terms, could find scope to live in health and dignity. The ways to do this are known; we have idle hands desperate for worthwhile work to do. Only the political will is lacking.

Let me conclude. We face, I fear, a future dominated by increasing scarcities in which the logic of the economic system will tend to concentrate even further wealth, income and power with the few and to polarise those who hold and control them from the rest of the community. I see that rest struggling to hold on to what they have – be it large or small – with concern for the weak and defenceless the commonest casualty. The strategy I have outlined cannot fundamentally change that future. It may mitigate its severity and give us time to come to terms with it. Only a dramatic reversal of the growth of human population could significantly affect the scarcities which confront us and our descendants.

But we are not inescapably dependent on this flood of commodities which our economic system is designed to produce. There are conceivable lifestyles more modest in their material demands, less destructive of the physical environment – lifestyles which are simpler, whose excitements are found primarily in the human relationships they provide scope for. The search for those lifestyles is the essential task of the rising generation. Upon their success in that search will depend the future of humankind.

Bibliography

Australia. Parliament. 1970. Senate Select Committee on Water Pollution in Australia (chairman: G.S. Davidson): *Report*. Canberra: Commonwealth Government Printer.

Australia. 1976. Royal Commission (chairman: H.C. Coombs). Australian Government Administration. Main report in series. Canberra: AGPS.

Australia. 1980. Committee of Inquiry into Technological Change in Australia (chairman: R.H. Myers). Canberra: AGPS.

Australia. Parliament. 1981. *Threats to Australia's Security: Their Nature and Probability*. Joint Committee on Foreign Affairs and Defence. Canberra: AGPS.

Australia. 1983. Department of Home Affairs and Environment. *Land Degradation in Australia* by L.E. Woods. Canberra: AGPS.

Australia. 1984. Department of Home Affairs and Environment. *National Strategy for Australia: Living Resource Conservation for Sustainable Development*. Proposed by a conference held in Canberra, June 1983. 2nd ed. Canberra: Canberra Publishing for Dept Home Affairs and Environment.

Ball, Desmond. 1980. *A Suitable Piece of Real Estate: American Installations in Australia*. Sydney: Hale & Iremonger.

Barker, R.G. 1974. 'Ecological Psychology: Concepts and Methods for Studying the Environment of Human Behaviour'. In Fox, K.A. (ed.) *Social Indicators and Social Theory*. New York: Wiley & Sons.

166

Bentham, J. 1789. *Introduction to the Principles of Morals and Legislation.*

Boulding, K.E. 1966. 'The Economics of the Coming Spaceship Earth'. In Jarrett, H. (ed.) *Environmental Quality in a Growing Economy.* Baltimore: Johns Hopkins Press.

Boulding, K.E. 1966. 'Economics and Ecology'. In Darling, F. and Milton, J.P. (eds) *Future Environments of North America.* New York: Natural History Press.

Boulding, K.E. 1971. 'Environment and Economics'. In Murdoch, W. (ed.) *Environment: Resources, Pollution and Society.* Stamford: Sinauer.

Bowlby, J. 1952. *Maternal Care and Infant Health.* Geneva: World Health Organisation.

Boyden, S.V. (ed.). 1970. *The Impact of Civilization on the Biology of Man.* Canberra: Australian National University Press.

Bunge, M. 1975. 'What is a quality of life indicator?' *Social Indicator Research* 2(1): 79.

Caldicott, H. 1978. *Nuclear Madness.* Milton, Queensland: Jacaranda Press.

Capital Territory, Department of. 1974. *Mine Waste Pollution of the Molonglo River.* Final Report on Remedial Measures June 1974. Joint Government Technical Committee on Mine Waste Pollution of the Molonglo River, June 1984. Canberra: AGPS.

Carrick, Sen. the Hon. Sir John and Steele, the Hon. Roger. 1983. *Rum Jungle Rehabilitation Program.* Joint press statement by Senator the Hon. Sir John Carrick, Minister for National Development and Energy, and the Hon. Roger Steele, Minister for Transport and Works for the Northern Territory. 2 March. Canberra.

Carson, R. 1962. *Silent Spring.* Boston: Houghton Mifflin.

Coelho, G.V., Hamburg, D.A. and Adams, J.E. 1974. *Coping and Adaptation.* New York: Basic Books Inc.

Commoner, B. 1971. *The Closing Circle.* New York: Alfred A. Knopf.

Commoner, B. (ed.) 1975. *Human Welfare – The End Use for Power.* New York: Macmillan Press.

Costin, A.B. and Frith, H.J. (eds) 1974. *Conservation* (rev. ed.). Harmondsworth: Penguin Books.

Dahlitz, J. 1983. *Nuclear Arms Control and Effective International Agreements.* Melbourne: McPhee Gribble.

Daly, H.E. (ed.) 1973. *Economics, Ecology, Ethics: Essays Towards a Steady State Economy.* San Francisco: W.H. Freeman.

Davy, D.R. (ed.). 1975. *Rum Jungle Environmental Studies.* Australian Atomic Energy Commission Research Establishment.

167

Diesendorf, M. (ed.). 1976. *The Magic Bullet*. Canberra: Society for Social Responsibility in Science, ACT.

Diesendorf, M. and Furnass, B. 1976. *The Impact of Environment and Life Style on Human Health*. Canberra: Society for Social Responsibility in Science, ACT.

Dobzhansky, T. 1962. *Mankind Evolving: The Evolution of the Human Species*. New Haven: Yale University Press.

Dubos, R. 1965. *Man Adapting*. New Haven, Conn.: Yale University Press.

Ehrman, L. and Parsons, P.A. 1976. *The Genetics of Behavior*. Massachusetts: Sinauer Associates Inc.

Fox, K.A. (ed.). 1974. *Social Indicators and Social Theory*. New York: Wiley & Sons.

Furnass, B. 1976. 'Adaptation: Ancient and Modern'. In Diesendorf, M. and Furnass, B. (eds). *The Impact of Environment and Lifestyle and Human Health*. Canberra: Society for Social Responsibility in Science, ACT.

Galbraith, J.K. 1958. *The Affluent Society*. Boston: Houghton Mifflin.

George, H. 1951. *Progress and Poverty*. New York: Robert Schalkenbach Foundation.

Georgescu, Roegen N. 1952. 'Toward a Partial Redirection of Econometrics', Part III. *Review of Economics and Statistics*. 34(4): 206–11.

Georgescu, Roegen N. 1969. 'Process in Farming versus Process in Manufacturing: A Problem of Balanced Development'. In Papi, U. and Nunn, C. (eds) *Economic Problems of Agriculture in Industrial Societies*. New York: St Martin's Press.

Georgescu, Roegen N. 1971. *The Entropy Law and the Economic Process*. Cambridge, Mass.: Harvard University Press.

Ginsberg, H. and Opper S. 1969. *Piaget's Theory of Intellectual Development*. London: Prentice Hall.

Gould, R. 1969. *Yiwara Foragers of the Australian Desert*. London: Collins.

Hall, T. 1980. *Darwin 1942*. Sydney: Methuen Australia.

Hardin, G. 1980. 'The Tragedy of the Commons'. In Daly, H.E. (ed.) *Economics, Ecology, Ethics: Towards a Steady-state Economy*. San Francisco: W.H. Freeman.

Henderson, H. 1980. *Creating Alternative Futures: The End of Economics*. New York: Perigee Books.

Hinchcliff, J. (ed). 1981. *Confronting the Nuclear Age – Australian Responses*. Bondi Junction, NSW: Pacific Peacemaker.

Hirsch, F. 1977. *Social Limits to Growth*. London: Routledge & Kegan Paul.

Ikle, F.C. 1958. *The Social Impact of Bomb Destruction*. Norman, Oklahoma: University of Oklahoma Press.

Illich, I. 1973. *Tools for Conviviality*. London: Calder & Boyars.

International Union for Conservation of Nature and Natural Resources. 1980. *World Conservation Strategy: Living Resource Conservation for Sustainable Development*. Gland, Switzerland: IUCN.

Jaspers, Karl. 1953. *The Origin and Goal of History*. London: Routledge & Kegan Paul.

Jevons, W.S. 1865. *The Coal Question*.

Johnson, H.G. 1973. *Man and His Environment*. London: The British–North American Committee.

Jones, R. 1969. 'Fire-Stick Farming'. *Australian Natural History* 16(7): 224–28.

Katz, A.M. 1982. *Life after Nuclear War: The Economic and Social Impacts of Nuclear Attacks on the United States*. Cambridge, Mass.: Ballinger Press.

Keynes, J.M. 1936. *The General Theory of Employment, Interest and Money*. London: Macmillan.

Keynes, J.M. 1963. 'Economic Possibilities for our Grandchildren'. In *Essays in Persuasion*, New York: Norton (originally published 1931).

Kuhn, T.S. 1970. *The Structure of Scientific Revolutions*. Chicago: University of Chicago Press.

Lawick-Goodall, J. von. 1970. *In the Shadow of Man*. London: Collins.

Leiss, W. 1978. *The Limits of Satisfaction*. London: Marion Boyars, London.

Lyons, 1975. *New Horizons in Linguistics*. Harmondsworth: Penguin Books.

Malthus, T.R. 1798. *An Essay on the Principle of Population*.

Marshall, A.J. (ed.). 1966. *The Great Extermination*. London: Heinemann.

Marx, K. 1867. *Capital*.

Meadows, D.H. *et al.* 1972. *The Limits to Growth*. A Report for the Club of Rome's Project on the Predicament of Mankind. New York: Universe Books.

Mill, J.S. 1859. *On Liberty*.

Mill, J.S. 1848, 1852. *Principles of Political Economy*.

Mishan, E.J. 1967. *The Costs of Economic Growth*. New York: Praeger.

Mishan, E.J. 1970. *Technology and Growth: The Price We Pay*. New York: Praeger.

Mishan, E.J. 1980. 'The growth of affluence and the decline of welfare'. In Daly, H.E. (ed.) *Economics, Ecology, Ethics: Essays Toward a Steady-state Economy*. San Francisco: W.H. Freeman.

Mumford, L. 1970. *The Myth of the Machine: Pentagon of Power*. London: Secker & Warburg.

169

Odum, E.P. 1969. 'The Strategy of Ecosystem Development'. In *Science*. 18 April 1969.

Ohlin, G. 1967. *Population Control and Economic Development*. Paris: Development Centre of the Organization for Economic Co-operation and Development.

Oldfield, R.C., and Marshall, J.C. (eds). 1969. *Language*. Harmondsworth: Penguin Books.

Packard, V. 1963. *The Waste Makers*. New York: Pocket Books.

Polanyi, K. 1968. 'Our Obsolete Market Mentality'. Reprinted in Dalton, G. (ed.) *Primitive, Archaic and Modern Economies: Essays of Karl Polanyi*. New York: Anchor Books.

Repetto, R.C. 1985. *The Global Possible: Resources, Development and the New Century*. New Haven, Conn.: Yale University Press.

Richelson, J. In press. 'Strategic nuclear targeting'. In Ball, D. and Richelson, J. (eds). *Assessment of the Post-attack Environment*. Chapter 13.

Robbins, L. 1932. *An Essay on the Nature and Significance of Economic Science*. London: Macmillan.

Robinson, J. 1962. *Economic Philosophy*. London: Watts.

Rowley, C.D. 1970. *The Destruction of Aboriginal Society*. Harmondsworth: Penguin.

Science Council of Canada. 1977. *Canada as a Conserver Society: Resource Uncertainties and the Need for New Technologies*. Report No. 27. Ottawa: Canadian Government Publishing Centre.

Science Council of Canada. 1979. *Forging the Links: A Technology Policy for Canada*. Report No. 29. Ottawa: Canadian Government Publishing Centre.

Shonfield, A. and Shaw, S. 1972. *Social Indicators and Social Policy*. London: Heinemann Educational Books.

Schumacher, E.F. 1964. 'Industrialization through Intermediate Technology'. In Chebbi, V. and McRobie, G. (eds) *Minerals and Industries*. Vol. 1(4). Calcutta: SIET Institute Hyderabad.

Schumacher, E.F. 1968. 'Buddhist Economics', *Resurgence*, Volume I(II). January–February 1968.

Schumacher, E.F. 1977. *A Guide for the Perplexed*. London: Jonathan Cape.

Schumacher, E.F. 1980. 'The Age of Plenty: A Christian View'. In Daly, H.E. (ed.) *Economics, Ecology, Ethics: Towards a Steady-state Economy*. San Francisco: W.H. Freeman.

Slatyer, R.O. 1970. *Man and the New Biology*. Canberra: Australian National University Press.

Stanner, W.E.H. 1968. 'After the Dreaming'. The Boyer Lectures. Sydney, Australian Broadcasting Commission.

Tawney, R.H. 1920. *The Acquisitive Society*. New York: Mentor.

Tawney, R.H. 1954. *Religion and the Rise of Capitalism*. New York: Mentor.

Valaskakis, K. *et al.* 1979. *The Conserver Society: A Workable Alternative for the Future*. New York: Harper & Row.

Wilcox, L.D., *et al.* 1972. *Social Indicators and Societal Monitoring*. Amsterdam: Elsevier.

Williams, H. 1973. *My Love had a Black Speed Stripe*. Melbourne: Macmillan.

Winter, J.M. and Joslin, D.M. (eds). 1972. *R.H. Tawney's Commonplace Book*. Cambridge, UK: Cambridge University Press.

Woodward, A.E. 1973-74. Aboriginal Land Rights Commission. First and Second Reports. Canberra: AGPS.

World Health Organisation. 1956. 'Study Group on the Psychobiological Development of the Child'. Tanner, J.M. and Inhelder, B. (eds). *Discussions on Child Development: Proceedings of the 4th Meeting*. London: Tavistock.

Wright, J. 1975. *Because I was Invited*. Melbourne: Oxford University Press.